P9-DGO-171

*Also by Ernst Pawel*

THE ISLAND IN TIME

FROM THE DARK TOWER

IN THE ABSENCE OF MAGIC

THE NIGHTMARE OF REASON:
A LIFE OF FRANZ KAFKA

THE LABYRINTH OF EXILE:
A LIFE OF THEODOR HERZL

LIFE IN DARK AGES:
A MEMOIR

# The Poet Dying

# THE

# POET

# DYING

## *Heinrich Heine's*

## *Last Years in Paris*

## *Ernst Pawel*

FARRAR, STRAUS AND GIROUX

NEW YORK

Copyright © 1995 by the estate of Ernst Pawel
All rights reserved
Printed in the United States of America
Published in Canada by HarperCollinsCanadaLtd
First edition, 1995

Library of Congress Cataloging-in-Publication Data
Pawel, Ernst.
The poet dying: Heinrich Heine's last years in Paris / Ernst
Pawel.—1st ed.
p.   cm.
Includes bibliographical references.
1. Heine, Heinrich, 1797–1856—Last years.   2. Heine, Heinrich,
1797–1856—Homes and haunts—France—Paris.   3. Authors,
German—19th century—Biography.   I. Title.
PT2332.P39  1995     831'.7—dc20 [B]     94–40744   CIP

Frontispiece: pencil portrait of Heine
by Marcellin-Gilbert Desboutin, ca. 1853,
used with permission of Heinrich-Heine-Institut, Düsseldorf

# Contents

## The Poet Dying 3

*A Selection of Heinrich Heine's Poems
in German and English*

### Romanzero

### Poems of 1853 and 1854

# The Poet Dying

THE CLOTTED MIX of sanctimonious respect and un-varnished glee with which, in the summer of 1847, several German newspapers reported the death of Heinrich Heine reflected not only the wishful thinking of those who, out of malice or gullibility, concocted these premature obits but also the exceedingly ambiguous position which Heine himself had occupied for so long in the world of both letters and politics. Indisputably Germany's most popular poet since the death of Goethe, he was also a man who had consistently gone out of his way to provoke the hostility of friend and foe alike.

Heine's genius for making enemies, intimately linked though it may have been to his poetic inspiration, proved a more than problematic gift throughout much of his life. A polemicist of matchless skill, he parried attacks with a virulent overkill that in at least two celebrated instances backfired badly and gained his opponents far more sympathy than they deserved. He regularly tended, moreover, to let himself be carried away by an exuberant sense of either justice or irony, or both, to the point of lashing out wildly and wittily without much regard as to choice of targets. These lightning and often preemptive strikes, his decided preference for smiting other cheeks rather than turning his own, constituted a clear and, to his contemporaries, decidedly alarming break with the age-old Jewish tradition of passivity in the face of aggression. Yet even without any deliberate effort on his part Heine would have had no trouble antagonizing a broad range of the German public across the entire political spectrum merely by virtue of being himself.

It was, on the face of it, a self riven by deep inner conflict and maddening outward contradictions, yet with a solid identity at the core; beyond the radical who dreaded revolution and the monarchist who sneered at kings, Heine was a poet first, last, and always, even in his essays and prolific journalism. And it is the almost playful power, the stunning versatility of his language, that ultimately mark him as profoundly subversive, regardless of sporadic efforts on his part to appear otherwise. The provocative simplicity and biting wit which he brought to German prose as well as poetry raised a direct challenge to the traditions of Teutonic pomposity, and the stolid Christian citizens of what with perverse tenacity he insisted on claiming as his fatherland felt duly outraged by what they correctly perceived as the intrusion of an alien spirit. His books were banned, one reason why they sold as well as they did; he himself was driven into exile, one reason why he never stopped pining for a land in which he could not bear to live.

•

This particular report of Heine's death turned out to have been somewhat exaggerated, although it circulated at a time when both he and his physicians expected the end to be imminent. Already in April he had "damn miserable nights, with a chest full of gurgling noises; if I didn't have a wife and a parrot, I would (may God forgive me) put an end to my misery like an ancient Roman." Had he known that the agony was to last another eight years, he might have overcome his scruples.

Some mystery or deliberate mystification surrounds Heine's date of birth, variously reported as December of either 1797 or 1799. All official records were destroyed in a series of fires; he himself insisted on the later date but in any case would at most have been only forty-nine years old when his illness entered its final and most devastating phase.

The exact nature of that illness has been the subject of much speculation and controversy. The first symptoms—a transient paralysis of the eyelids and two fingers—seem to have manifested themselves as early as 1831, but even during his student days Heine had already begun to suffer from the crippling headaches seen by some experts as pointing to a possibly hereditary ailment. In 1837, his vision was affected so severely that he feared imminent blindness; although he temporarily recovered, the visual disturbances recurred episodically as the illness progressed. His complaints, in 1843, of a left facial paralysis and numbness in the left extremities raise strong suspicions of a stroke, but the most abrupt deterioration in his health took place immediately following the death, in December 1844, of Uncle Salomon, the multimillionaire brother of his own feckless and impecunious father. The long struggle between the uncle, an imperious philistine—"You wouldn't have to write poetry if you'd learned a proper trade"—on whose financial support Heine and his family depended, and the arrogant nephew—"Your only claim to fame is that you bear my name"—took on all the violent ambivalence of an Oedipal confrontation with its full load of emotional ramifications. Formal notice that the uncle had cut him entirely out of his will and that even the regular annual subsidy would no longer be forthcoming was a shock so severe that Heine blamed it, probably with some justification, for the dramatic worsening of his condition. He spent the summer of 1845 in the sulfur baths at Montmorency doctoring an all but unbearable rash and was stricken the following spring with a glottal paralysis that eventually spread to the lower extremities. Up until the end of 1847, however, he still experienced repeated remissions and was on occasion able to leave the house, although Engels, after a visit, reported to Marx that it was "sad to see such a splendid fellow die bit by bit." But after his total collapse in early February

1848, Heine, racked by bouts of excruciating pain, his lower extremities as well as his eyelids paralyzed and with only minimal control of his arms, never again left his room and remained buried more or less alive in his "mattress tomb" until his death eight years later, on February 17, 1856. They were eight years of unremitting torture, during which he produced some of his greatest and most moving work.

Heine's doctors at the time lacked both the tools and the knowledge for a definitive diagnosis, which did not, of course, keep them from propounding their authoritative opinions with the same zealotry with which they proceeded to apply treatments ranging from leeches, enemas, and cauterization of the spine to opium rubbed into sores deliberately kept open. Heine himself, *faute de mieux* echoing their view, referred to his illness as a degenerative disease of the spine due to a syphilitic infection, a view not seriously challenged until nearly a century after his death, when a number of experts raised questions about the diagnosis and suggested alternatives. To begin with, while Heine remained demonstrably lucid and remarkably serene to the very last day of his life, it seems exceedingly rare for a syphilitic disease to reach an advanced stage such as, in this instance, *tabes dorsalis*, without gravely affecting the mental faculties and emotional stability of the patient. Moreover, from 1834 to his death, Heine lived with Crescence Eugénie Mirat—immortalized by him as Mathilde—in what certainly was no platonic relationship; yet Mathilde, whom he married in 1843 in a proper Catholic ceremony, survived in provocatively robust health until 1883.

A number of alternative diagnostic hypotheses have since been put forward; they include congenital neuropathy, porphyria, or, more plausibly, amyotrophic lateral sclerosis and a number of muscular dystrophies. None of which is of more than academic interest or in any way affects our view of this 70-pound skeleton who, nearly sightless, heavily sedated, often unable to speak beyond a whisper, managed throughout this interminable season in hell to produce a steady stream of powerful poetry and matchless prose.

Testimony to the—occasionally—transcendent grandeur of the human spirit, the more surprising in that up to the onset of his illness, or rather the appearance of its first serious symptoms in his early forties, Heine in his letters and polemical writings as well as in the accounts of many of his contemporaries emerges as a monstrous egotist, sure of his genius but constantly preoccupied with problems of health, fame, and money. The metamorphosis of this rather strident hypochondriac into a long-suffering near-saint hints at emotional and intellectual resources far beyond anything even he himself suspected: "The most horrible despair, along with emotional and physical torture which, however, I bear with a serenity of which I would have never believed myself capable."

But by isolating and ultimately all but sealing him off from the world at large, the illness also symbolized in gruesome and climactic extreme Heine's lifelong destiny as the quintessential outsider.

•

He was a bad fit from the outset, a cuckoo's egg, the poetic genius inexplicably hatched in the thoroughly prosaic milieu of the petty-minded bourgeoisie. In his uncle's millionaire establishment the teenage Harry—the name inflicted upon him at birth—was the ugly duckling, the dunce who, unable to add up a column of figures, had the temerity instead to fall in love with the daughter of the house. At the university he wrote German poetry instead of studying Roman law. The poetry brought fame, the prose brought notoriety. Irreverence and wit being *verboten* in his native land, the greatest German poet of his generation spent the last twenty-five years of his life in exile, his books banned, a warrant out for his arrest. In 1834 the Prussian Foreign Minister even went so far as to call for the death sentence.

Brash, unsparing, and lucid though it was, nothing Heine wrote would ever have quite justified this *furor teutonicus*. More than anything else, what really roiled Germany's politicians and churned the bowels of her patriots was that the greatest German poet of his generation happened to be a Jew.

The outsider by definition.

•

Seen from a post-Holocaust perspective, the assimilation of German Jewry, starting with Moses Mendelssohn in the late eighteenth century, may appear a disastrous failure, a painful process of self-deception culminating in the gas chambers. This somewhat simplistic view fails to account for the untold thousands of Jews who, in the course of two or three generations, shed their religious and cultural background so successfully as to vanish completely into the general population, proof that assimilation was indeed an option of sorts, at least up to the Nazi period. Heine's younger brother Gustav edited a conservative newspaper in Vienna, was knighted in recognition for his services to the government, and, adopting the mother's gentile-sounding maiden name, emerged as the Baron von Heine-Geldern. The youngest of the three brothers, a physician in the Russian Army, quite simply ennobled himself and retired in St. Petersburg as the Baron von Heine. Their sister Charlotte had to settle for an untitled husband of Jewish origin, but her son became a Baron von Emden, while her daughter married a Principe della Rocca. Within two generations, the entire Heine clan—including Uncle Salomon's offspring—had become thoroughly de-Judaized.

Assimilation, then, was indeed possible, but only for

those willing to fully surrender their identity and adopt the dominant culture; even the most philo-Semitic German liberals—and there were some—expected a Jew to stop being and acting like one as the price of admission to civilized society. It was a price Heine himself was both unable and unwilling to pay.

He had, like his other siblings, undergone conversion for purely practical reasons—in his case at the conclusion of his law studies, when, with a youthful lack of self-knowledge verging on the grotesque, he envisaged a diplomatic career for himself. To the atheist he was at the time, the act itself seemed a formality devoid of any spiritual significance, though he later came to regret it as a matter of principle. He lacked piety, observed no traditions, and would probably have been hard put to define his Judaism, yet his German critics were dead right when they read it into almost everything he ever wrote. The greatest German poet of his time was a Jew looking at the Germans from the outside, one reason why he saw them as clearly as he did.

The illness transformed the outsider by rapid stages into a hermit, a prisoner, a living mind entombed in an all but dead body. Or, as he himself put it in a public statement, "nothing anymore but a poor Jew, and a deadly ill one at that."

BY 1847 THE POLITICAL and economic pressures in France, and for that matter in most of Europe, were rapidly building to an explosive climax. But Heine, normally an astute and uncommonly sensitive observer, missed the storm signals in this particular instance. For which he may well be forgiven, considering his more personal problems.

He had been living in Paris since 1831, lured initially by what—briefly and from a distance—seemed like a reprise of the French Revolution of 1789. Throughout Europe, the dream of *liberté, égalité, fraternité* still worked its magic on those young enough or poor enough to welcome change, while those too old, too rich, or too wise were haunted by the nightmare of the guillotine.

As it happened, the revolution of 1830 fizzled within a matter of days, its anticlimactic outcome a largely cosmetic shuffle in which a stupid despot—Charles X—was replaced by a cunningly despotic one posing as a "citizen king." But Heine had other, ultimately far more cogent reasons for leaving Germany, an at the time still somewhat loose con-federation of petty tyrannies dominated by Prussia. In fact, as early as 1826 he wrote about wanting to turn his back on his native land. "What drives me out is not *Wanderlust* but the torment of personal relations, for instance the im-possibility of ever shedding the Jew." In the prevailing atmosphere of political reaction and Christian sanctimony, his prose was deemed subversive and his poetry obscene; and while the unremitting persecution by censors of various jurisdictions greatly enhanced his fame and notoriety, it also made life and work increasingly difficult for a writer congenitally unable to conform even in spite of occasionally genuine efforts to do so. In the spring of 1831, Prussia banned two of his new books outright, and he had reason to worry about possible criminal charges against him.

Paris, on the other hand, glittering metropolis of nearly a million, heart of the civilized world, gave a warm welcome to the already renowned poet and celebrated foe of tyranny when he arrived there on May 10. An instant celebrity, lionized by the literary and artistic establishment, he quickly felt, if not at home—he was not one to ever feel at home anywhere—at least "like a fish in the water. Or rather, tell people that if two fishes meet in the water and ask about each other's well-being, the proper answer should be: like Heine in Paris." What had been planned as an extended stay became a lifelong exile when, in 1835, the German Federal Assembly at the personal insistence of Metternich banned all of Heine's writings and the Prussian police issued a warrant for his arrest. Neither threat, in those idyllically pre-totalitarian and technologically backward times, was very effective—the books continued to be printed and sold, and Heine made two furtive, very brief trips to Germany in 1843 and 1844, but the fact remains that he spent the rest of his life in Paris. And no matter how often he deplored the fate of the exile and how eloquently he expressed his longings for the native soil, he remained in Paris because that was where he belonged, the most cosmopolitan city on earth and the one place where the outsider was an insider.

Besides, what were the alternatives? "When I think of Germany at night, I lose my sleep." Or the newly independent home of the brave and land of the free? "Go to America, where there are no lords and no aristocracy, where all men are equal, that is to say, equally boorish, except of course for several million people with black or brown skin

[*11*]

who are being treated like dogs. I am not nearly as outraged by the actual slavery, abolished in most northern provinces, as about the brutality with which the free blacks and mulattoes are being treated . . . At that, the Americans make a big show of their Christianity and are the most zealous of churchgoers, hypocrisy being what they learned from the British."

Written in 1836.

As exile went, Paris was benign.

•

Between his triumphant arrival in Paris and the unmistakable portents of his imminent physical collapse in 1847 lay sixteen years of extraordinary turmoil, achievement, controversy, scandal, success, failure, and the never-ending struggle to make ends meet. Money was an almost constant preoccupation to the day of his death, though the reasons are still far from clear. He was one of the first true freelancers determined to support himself by his writings, and as such also one of the first victims of greed and dishonesty on the part of his publisher. Moreover, under the then prevailing system, he sold his rights to each work for a lump sum rather than collecting royalties, thus deriving little profit from his vast popularity, while his publisher became a rich man. Even so, the income from his writing alone still added up to what for his day was a very respectable amount; in addition, he received substantial help from his much reviled wealthy relatives as well as an annual subsidy from the French government, benefits which ultimately cost him a great deal in self-respect and reputation but which nonetheless should have freed him from any acute financial distress, the more so since he lived very modestly in dingy, sparsely furnished apartments and indulged in no extravagant vices other than spontaneous generosity toward many of his fellow exiles, among whom he was widely known as a soft touch. But for a man as manifestly indifferent as he was to the things money could buy, he spent an inordinate amount of time and energy fretting about it; and while his illness in its final stages required large expenditures, he seemed to be constantly strapped for funds all through his Paris years.

The clue to this as to many another mystery in Heine's life is probably Mathilde.

Crescence Eugénie Mirat was nineteen—fifteen years younger than he—and a near-illiterate, orphaned shopgirl when first they met in 1834, one of a series of casual encounters he immortalized in a famous cycle of erotic poems. But the girl he renamed Mathilde, for reasons as obscure as so much else about this affair, instantly captivated him. She was a capricious child, moderately bright but innocent of even the most rudimentary education, and he loved the shape of her behind, yet there were obviously far more complex and largely unconscious reasons to account for an obsessive infatuation to which, after fighting it for a year, he was finally forced to yield. She moved in with him in 1836, he married her in 1841, and—happily or not—they lived together until his death. She loved shopping even more than she loved her parrot; she had no remote idea of her husband's place, fame, and achievements in the world at large, yet she stuck with him to the end, which was a great deal more than any of his friends expected or, for that matter, might have wished for. And he in turn fussed and worried about her financial future into his final hours— quite unnecessarily so, as it turned out; she showed far more business sense in disposing of his manuscripts after his death than he ever did in life.

•

The radiant lyricism of his early poetry, the venomous sarcasm of his prose, and the obdurate skepticism of his politics conspired to obscure an aspect of Heine's character which, though it found its overt expression only in the work of his final years, was a dark presence from the very beginning—a basically tragic sense of life. Buffoonery, self-righteousness, and seawater baths were among the tactics he used to shield himself as best he could from the corrosive impact of his own visions, but whether conscious or not, they lent depth and substance to much of what he wrote. The man who fancied himself the modern Aristophanes was always able to appreciate the wayward whimsy of the Ironist Supreme:

> *Lass die heil'gen Parabolen,*
> *Lass die frommen Hypothesen—*
> *Suche die verdammten Fragen*
> *Ohne Umschweif uns zu lösen.*
>
> *Warum schleppt sich blutend, elend,*
> *Unter Kreuzlast der Gerechte,*
> *Während glücklich als ein Sieger*
> *Trabt auf hohem Ross der Schlechte?*
>
> *Woran liegt die Schuld? Ist etwa*
> *Unser Herr nicht ganz allmächtig?*
> *Oder tribt er selbst den Unfug?*
> *Ach, das wäre niederträchtig.*
>
> *Also fragen wir beständig,*
> *Bis man uns mit einer Handvoll*
> *Erde endlich stopft die Mäuler—*
> *Aber ist das eine Antwort?*

*(Never mind the holy parables and pious hypotheses*
*Give us an answer to these damn questions without beating*
*around the bush.*

*Why does the just man stagger bleeding and wretched under*
  *the weight of the cross*
*While the wicked, happy victor rides along on his high*
  *horse?*

*Who's to blame? Could it be that our Lord is not almighty*
  *after all?*
*Or is this mischief his own doing?*
*That would be a dirty trick indeed.*

*And so we ask and keep on asking*
*Till in the end they stuff our mouth*
*With a handful of cold clay—*
*Is this what you call an answer?)\**

The man who wrote these lines cannot have been unduly
surprised by the intimations of imminent mortality in the
spring of 1847; his words breathe a defiance that probably
explains as well as anything the almost defiant serenity with
which Heine bore his cross and which he himself found
even more amazing than did those who had known him in
his earlier roles.

Heine considered himself the best-qualified mediator between France and Germany, the one writer sufficiently
conversant with both cultures to interpret one to the other.
There is some substance to his claim. He wrote for several
French and German newspapers, and what he brought to
his journalism over the years, aside from an acerbic wit and
an astonishingly modern sensibility, was a remarkable intuition that at times could seem downright prophetic, as

* The translations in the text of this book were done by Ernst Pawel
and therefore differ slightly from the translations in the Selection of Poems
which begins on page 195.

plain common sense often has a way of doing. Neither his *Conditions in France* nor his *De l'Allemagne* (the title a takeoff on Mme de Staël's celebrated opus, which he detested) contains the sort of ponderous punditry that marks most deep thinkers as blithering bores; the books were bestsellers in their day and are still eminently readable, no small achievement and a tribute to his unique style.

But this impressionistic approach has its obvious limitations, and the fact is that in the course of his sixteen-year exile Heine had quite lost touch with the situation in Germany without ever becoming truly French in spirit, manner, or language. Thus, for instance, although he grew up hearing French in his native Düsseldorf, he retained a strong German accent and seldom trusted himself to write in French. And while he had a wide net of acquaintances among the elite of French politics and the arts, he made few close or lasting friends. As for the common folk, there was only Mathilde and her own peculiar social set; Marx suspected them all of being pimps and prostitutes, but the old curmudgeon's judgment has been somewhat discredited of late.

Heine's other circle was the semi-permanent colony of German political exiles, often up to about 40,000 at a time, divided into groups and grouplets led by men like Börne, Herwegh, Lasalle, and Marx. Over time, Heine managed to alienate each and every one of them (except for Marx, who appreciated him as a poet but did not take him seriously as a political thinker). "The local German Jacobins . . . want to force me to declare myself *for* or *against* them, whereas I have thus far refused to do the first out of conviction and the second out of wisdom. I am not the sort of person who lets himself be forced to take a stand, and all they've achieved is to make me more moderate than ever out of disgust with their Jacobin dishonesty."

Needless to say, this attitude did not sit well with most of the firebrands of the German emigration, who were quick to accuse him of fence-sitting. The charge was justified to some extent, but what made Heine so frequently resist commitment even to causes he basically believed in was skepticism rather than opportunism, the nasty habit of the neo-Talmudist to counter each answer with at least two new questions. As early as the 1840s he saw a Communist revolution as both inevitable and potentially devastating, but he despised the cabal of self-styled leaders who spent their days plotting it in the cafés of Montmartre, and the barbed sarcasm with which he customarily expressed his contempt did not enhance his popularity among the exiled vanguard of Germany's forthcoming liberation. At the very most, he commanded a measure of respect; whether he ever needed or expected more is an open question.

•

By 1847, the "citizen king" Louis Philippe had confirmed Heine's earlier suspicions and revealed himself as a rigid demagogue determined to revive the absolutist practices of his Bourbon ancestors. Thus it came to pass that half a century after the revolution proclaiming the Rights of Man, French election laws stipulated a poll tax of minimally 200 francs. With a craftsman earning about 600 francs a year and an ordinary worker about half that amount, all but some 250,000 voters out of a male adult population of 9 million were effectively disenfranchised. And as the demands for electoral reforms grew ever more clamorous, Prime Minister Guizot defended the tax in a manner fatally reminiscent of Marie Antoinette's crack about eating cake: "You want to vote, all you have to do is get rich."

He did, and so did a few thousand other crooks and racketeers. France was rife with corruption from top to bottom; even the wine was universally being adulterated, to the point where the export of French brands became virtually impossible. But while the unfairness of the electoral laws fueled the indignation of the bourgeoisie, the working class had other, more pressing concerns, such as widespread unemployment, starvation wages, lack of sanitation, and living conditions in general still mired in the Middle Ages as France—at a pace second only to England's—underwent the painful transition from an agricultural to an industrialized society. In a humanitarian gesture analogous to his comment on electoral reform, Guizot sponsored a law limiting child labor to twelve hours a day and banning it altogether for children under the age of eight.

It would have been difficult to ignore the approaching crisis. In the Chamber of Deputies, the arch-conservative Alexis de Tocqueville warned that "a wind of revolution blows, the storm is on the horizon," while at the other end of the political spectrum, Marx and Engels published the *Communist Manifesto* in late 1847. Heine himself had frequently delivered himself of apocalyptic prophecies, at first with revolutionary fervor and later with nuanced apprehension. For sixteen years he had observed and written about the France of Louis Philippe from the viewpoint of a privileged outsider—privileged in the sense of having an insider's access to the top levels of government and culture. In his reports for the *Augsburger Allgemeine Zeitung*, later revised and published in book form, his intuitive, highly subjective approach to politics and the arts yielded brilliant insights as well as strong opinions, along with a fair measure of banal chatter, but never any consistent point of view. And while there are many pragmatic reasons for the vacillating, multifaceted ambiguities in his attitude toward the king, his government, the mood of the masses, and the politics of revolution, the most fundamental one was quite simply an aspect of Heine's character. He for one saw nothing inconsistent in being on several sides of an issue, but a certain naïveté in this as well as in some other respects also helped to keep him young in spirit.

In 1847, however, he failed to read the signs altogether. Understandably enough, as the paralysis gained on him, other more abstract and less personal concerns shrank correspondingly. But it is also true that after all his years in Paris he no longer had the newcomer's acute perceptions and perspectives; on the one hand, he was himself too much part of the scene to notice the mood shifting all around him, and on the other, he let his judgment all too frequently be swayed by his close contacts with the leaders of the government, all of whom chose to either minimize the gravity of the situation or to ignore it altogether.

And in any case, what Heine most wanted, in the spring of 1847, was to regain his health and either live or die.

IN DUE COURSE of time the exiled *enfant terrible* of German letters had become one of the more esoteric tourist attractions of the French capital, an obligatory stop on the sightseeing circuit for visitors from beyond the Rhine, who ranged from curious fools, celebrity hunters, and assorted freaks to literary or political conspirators. On the whole, Heine welcomed these visits, no matter how volubly he complained about them; aside from reassuring him about his continuing fame and stature back home, they kept him up-to-date on literary gossip and intrigue.

Many of these visitors left a record of their impressions, among the most detailed being the memoirs of Alfred Meissner, a versatile Prague *littérateur*, author of a number of poems, plays, and novels, but now remembered only for his recollections of Heine. Their reliability has been called into question, no doubt justifiably so, memory being inherently creative even where no secondary gain is involved. Marx went one step further; in a letter to Engels written after Heine's death, he accuses "the worthy Meissner, who had peddled so much cowshit to the German public," of having received money from Mathilde "to glorify this human swine who had tormented Heine to death." Heine himself, on the other hand, liked the young man from the very beginning, thought rather highly of his gifts, and—a rare case among his acquaintances and perhaps a tribute to Meissner's tact—remained on friendly terms with him to the very end. This does not make Meissner's testimony any more or less suspect than that of Heine's enemies, but it did give him fuller access in the later years.

Their first meeting took place on February 10, 1847, when the then twenty-five-year-old climbed the "three wooden, narrow, smoothly polished and dangerously slippery" flights of stairs to Heine's apartment at 46, rue Faubourg Poissonnière, in the Ninth Arrondissement. "The apartment of one of Germany's greatest poets of all time was certainly vastly inferior to that of any second- or third-rate French author. Three tiny rooms on the third floor furnished with very modest comfort. The view, if that is the word, was of a dark and narrow courtyard. The fireplace had the usual marble facing, with a wide mirror above it; the clock ticking away noisily in its porcelain housing between the—in France inevitable—vases filled with artificial flowers was the one most conspicuous piece of decoration."

As Meissner remembers it, Heine at the time was still "far from being the sick man of his later years. True, the right eye was shut, but other traces of the earlier stroke were barely noticeable in his face. It was a face of peculiar beauty, a high and noble forehead, the nose finely molded, a delicate mouth hidden within a beard that also covered the entire chin. The beard was already speckled with white, whereas the full brown hair, which hung far down to his neck, did not yet betray any traces of age. The total impression was one of wistful melancholy, yet once he started to move or to speak, a surge of unsuspected energy and a surprising, almost fiendish smile took over. He was still fairly mobile on his legs and able, if he wanted to get hold of a newspaper article, to walk all the way from Faubourg Poissonnière to the *cabinet de lecture* at the Palais Royal."

But five months earlier, on September 19, 1846, Engels in a letter to Marx had described Heine's condition in far more ominous terms: "The poor devil is going to the dogs. Thin as a rail, the softening of the brain spreading, and so is the facial paralysis . . . He could die suddenly of pneumonia or a stroke, but he could also linger on for some three or four more years. He is naturally somewhat depressed, melancholy, and—a rather significant change—exceedingly restrained in his judgments . . . Otherwise still full of energy intellectually, but his appearance, rendered even more weird by the graying beard (he cannot bear a razor around his mouth) is enough to sadden everyone who sees him."

The discrepancy is probably more apparent than real in that the progress of Heine's illness, though inexorable, was marked by repeated if increasingly brief remissions over the course of the years, and in the spring of 1847 he seems to have been in relatively good shape—for the very last time, as it turned out. Alexandre Weill, an Alsatian Jewish author more renowned for his gossip than his writings, describes a luncheon he hosted early in the year for Heine, Balzac, and Eugène Sue. Sue, a physician turned novelist, had published a series of immensely popular novels, *Les Mystères de Paris*, *Le Juif errant*, *Les Sept Péchés capitaux* being among the best known; his prolific output and his passionate commitment to social reform invited comparisons with Dickens. Four years younger than Heine, he was most eager to meet the celebrated German rebel, but Balzac initially balked; although on friendly terms with Heine, the author of the *Comédie humaine*—posthumously transformed into a quasi-Marxist critic of capitalism—in fact despised socialism in general and Sue's type of social activism in particular. Eventually, however, a three-hour meeting did take place, and if Weill's extensive notes can be trusted, Balzac dominated the occasion. He opened the discussion by declaring, with a regal flourish, that his opinions were well known. "They are old. But truth does not have to be new. Nor am I unaware of the chinks in my armor, which my friend Heine in any case would be quick to discover. What I intend to prove—and this is why I came—is that the so-called new is false, a complete chimera . . . Let me tell you that socialism, which thinks of itself as new, is in fact old hat, a parricide that has always killed the republic, its mother, and freedom, its sister . . . the ancient struggle between grace and liberty, between Plato and Aristotle, between St. Augustin and St. Thomas."

Except for an occasional caustic remark, Heine apparently kept out of the increasingly heated argument between the two combative novelists, until they finally insisted that he state his own opinion. "As a German," he said, "I of course have several at once. But let me summarize them . . . I note that the 24-hour day consists of a day and a night—two opposites. A day without a night, however beautiful, would be decidedly inconvenient. I also note that in order to have a child you need a man and a woman, two further opposites that sometimes join with a certain measure of harmony. Next, to do business, you need an idiot and a smart man. I was told—by Berlioz, I think, since Meyerbeer is mad at me—that the common chord consists of a third, a fifth, and an octave, a mystery which the cabalists have applied to love as well . . . In short, everything that endures, that gives pleasure, consists of opposites. I think the same applies to the problem of the republic versus the monarchy. What we need is not one or the other but both simultaneously . . . a republic ruled by monarchists, or a monarchy ruled by republicans. I could give you fifty further irrefutable arguments in support of my thesis . . . but I must stop here, because I have a wife. Or rather, my wife has me, and she will never believe that I had lunch with literary geniuses. I have to get home, and hope to see you soon at my house. We'll proclaim the republic. Balzac will be President, Sue the Secretary General. I shall put your glory into German verses, Meyerbeer will set them to music, and little Weill here, who has a good tenor voice, will sing them."

Whether or not Weill's notes were accurate to the letter,

they certainly caught the spirit of Heine's ambivalence about the grand political issues of his day. The three writers were never to meet again; Balzac died in 1850, at the age of fifty-one, and Sue outlived Heine by barely a year.

•

The ambivalence, of course, went back to beginnings; Heine had always been rebel rather than revolutionary, naysayer rather than would-be prophet, even during his politically most radical phase, which roughly coincided with Marx's presence in Paris, from 1843 to 1845. The line was blurred by the fact that he and the left-wing radicals had so many enemies in common. But whereas the Communists *believed*—whether in the collective wisdom of the proletariat, the redemptive potential of the revolution, or whatever—Heine never for a moment shed his skepticism. His was an essentially bleak view which, the world being what it is, made for considerably more accurate predictions than the revolutionary optimism of his radical sometime-friends.

But if this skepticism was all too often seen as out-and-out cynicism, the fault was largely Heine's own; he could seldom resist a witticism or a sarcastic crack, no matter who or what the target. Writing in the *Revue des Deux Mondes* in 1844, Marie d'Agoult, Liszt's lover and herself the hostess of a famous salon, said of Heine that "in verse as in prose, he has mocked God and all the divinities. No belief, no sentiment, no idea has ever stirred him to fervor or enthusiasm; he has made fun of his fatherland, of love, of art, of nature, of his friends, his relatives, and of himself." This summary judgment on the part of the German-born, convent-bred Mme Agoult, about whom Heine had at least as many reservations as he did about her lover, quite accurately reflects the impression he made and perhaps deliberately cultivated in society, but it does not touch on the essence of the man. The difference between a skeptic and a cynic may escape the myopic eye, but however slight, it happens to be a crucial one.

Moreover, there was one commitment about which he never felt the slightest trace of ambivalence, and it, too, contributed to his isolation. During roughly the decade preceding 1848, the very same tensions that eventually led to the bloody uprisings in France, Germany, and Austria-Hungary also exerted a correspondingly profound influence on the sort of poetry and prose being written in those countries. Thus much of the writing perpetrated by German radicals during that period anticipated, albeit on a more modest scale, the experiments in socialist realism of our own century. Heine, on the other hand, was never willing to let political criteria overrule artistic ones. Nor, being Heine, would he ever deprive himself of the opportunity to lampoon those who did.

One result was the long—2,000-line—poem *Atta Troll*, which he worked on starting in 1842 and of which several fragments, badly mangled by censorship and editorial cuts, appeared in a German magazine the following year. He resumed work on it in 1844 but did not get it in shape for final publication until the beginning of 1847, when it appeared with a mordant preface attacking the radical colleagues—"the valiant champions of light and truth"—who back in the early forties had accused him of selling out and had now for the most part settled comfortably into smugness, patriotism, and civil service, whereas he, with warrants outstanding for his arrest at every customs station along the German border, would conclude his life in exile.

The so-called art of political poetry was flourishing at the time *Atta Troll* was conceived [he wrote]. The Muses received strict orders henceforth not to go about frolicking idly and frivolously anymore but to enroll in the service of the fatherland, be it as sutlers peddling liberty or as washerwomen laundering the Christian-Germanic nationhood. What most especially erupted in the groves of German poetry was this sterile pathos, this pointless miasmic enthusiasm plunging . . . into an ocean of platitudes . . . Talent, in those days, was a decidedly suspect gift in that it was equated with lack of character. Envious impotence . . . had at last come up with a powerful weapon against the insolence of genius: it discovered the antithesis of talent versus character. The masses found it personally flattering to be told that while good people as a rule were bad musicians, good musicians were usually anything but good people, and what really counted in this world was goodness rather than music. The empty head bragged about the good heart, and attitude was the decisive asset. I remember a writer of that period proud of the fact that he couldn't write; he was awarded a silver cup for his wooden prose.

*Atta Troll*, a poem in unrhymed trochaic tetrameter, is an animal fable, at the time a popular genre for purposes of satire. Its eponymous hero, a shaggy, malodorous bear whose pathetic little dance makes him think of himself as a major artist, is a pompous, puritanical radical who, having escaped from captivity, takes to the woods to preach the rebellion of the animals against the rights of man. He embodies everything Heine despised about the radical literati of the period: their vapid rhetoric, self-importance, chauvinism, narrow-minded moralism, and insipid anthropocentric, or in this instance ursopocentric, religiosity, Atta Troll's god being the Great White Polar Bear in the sky. The hunt for the rebellious escapee, in which the human narrator plays a reluctant and subsidiary role, expands into a series of wild allegorical fantasies which, with a characteristic blend of playfulness, irony, and melancholy, touch upon some of the conflicts—realism versus romanticism, Hellenic spirit versus Judaic tradition—Heine was never

[26]

really able to resolve to his own satisfaction. Even more to the point, though, is the lucidly dramatized confrontation of Enlightenment humanism with the righteous claims of the repressed masses. Although emotionally committed to the first, he at the same time felt convinced that revolution, however deplorable in its ultimate effects, was not only justified but probably inevitable. The dancing bear's ringing call to arms against the oppressor, even while parodying the vapid rhetoric of his human counterparts, contains enough persuasive arguments to lend considerable inner tension to the poem.

Much of it is dissipated for the modern reader, familiar with neither the allusions, the Aesopian language, nor the contemporaries whom Heine set out to caricature. But at the time of its publication *Atta Troll*, though immediately banned in Germany, was again a huge success there and did quite well even in France, where it appeared in the *Revue des Deux Mondes* of March 15, 1847, in a translation by Edouard Grenier.

Yet Heine did much more than attack the dancing bears of political poetry; what lent his critique a special edge was that he, for one, practiced what he preached. His own songs, though popular among the increasingly mutinous German workers, never condescended to the bathos of proletarian patriotism, the outstanding example being "The Silesian Weavers," one of the most haunting revolutionary poems ever written. Inspired by the first organized working-class uprising in Germany—the strike of the desperate Silesian weavers of Peterswaldau in 1844—it remains a rare achievement of its kind, an impassioned protest and political indictment that draws its poignant emotional force from the sheer power of its language.

•

Even in the best of circumstances Heine had never been a facile writer, but during the two years of the "inheritance feud"—from the death of his uncle Salomon in December 1844 to February 1847—his total output added up to little more than the preface to *Atta Troll* and a ballet scenario commissioned by Benjamin Lumley, director of Her Majesty's Theater in London. It was Heine's version of the Faust legend, but although Lumley paid him the generous sum of 6,000 francs, he regretfully found himself unable, on technical as well as moral grounds, to produce it in a theater frequently attended by Queen Victoria.

The inheritance feud was formally settled by what passed for a reconciliation of sorts between Heine and his cousin Carl, who agreed to pay him a pension for life, with half the amount—2,400 francs annually—payable to Mathilde after his death, provided he publish nothing about any members of even the extended Heine family. Gossip, some of it circulated by Heine himself, has tried to explain cousin Carl's all-too-effective blackmail as an act of jealous revenge for an affair his French wife supposedly had with the poet long before her marriage, but the petty mind of an arrogant, exquisitely stupid philistine of enormous wealth would seem a more than adequate explanation for Carl Heine's behavior. In any event, it may account for the disappearance of the famous memoirs that Heine talked about for years; apparently he burned much of what he had written for fear that their posthumous publication would cause cousin Carl to stop supporting the widowed Mathilde. And Mathilde herself, ignorant of German, seems to have turned some manuscripts in her possession over to the family after Heine's death; at any rate, no trace of any memoirs has been found.

•

If the worries about his widow's future led to a number of regrettable compromises, they also provided a much needed incentive for him to keep on working in defiance of his illness. "She is so spoiled and so inexperienced that I simply cannot provide enough for her," he wrote to his mother in February 1847. "If she were smarter, I'd worry less about her future. Which again goes to show that stupidity is a gift of the gods, because it forces others to take care of you."

He did his best for her, part of his efforts consisting of occasionally rather risky investments. The stock exchange crash of 1847 caused him considerable losses but also seems to have given him some basic insight into the reasons for his recurrent failures as a businessman. "You see," he told a friend on the morning after the disaster, "the Rabbi Ben Shloime of Prague turns out to have been right after all. It really comes down to an old story I heard as a boy. The rabbi is crossing the Charles Bridge when a Jewish woman comes running after him, screaming for help. 'What happened?' the rabbi wants to know. 'My son Yitzhak broke his leg.' 'How did he break his leg?' 'He climbed a ladder and wanted to . . .' 'What?' the rabbi cut her short. 'He climbed a ladder? Serves him right. What business does a Jew have climbing a ladder?' And this," Heine concluded, "applies to me, too. What business does a poet have investing in stocks?"

Sharing the nineteenth-century faith in the health benefits of fresh air and a change of scenery—the mud baths of the previous years had proved useless—Heine in mid-May moved into a rented cottage in Montmorency, a town of a few thousand inhabitants about ten miles north of Paris, where Jean-Jacques Rousseau had spent two years writing his *Nouvelle Héloïse*; it owed its popularity as a summer resort principally to a large forest with numerous bridle paths. He spent a relatively quiet summer there, unable to work because of persistent eye trouble but hosting a large number of visitors until the middle of September, when the paralysis began to spread alarmingly and he decided to return to his Paris apartment.

By the end of the year he was rarely able to leave the house, but one of his last excursions was described by Caroline Jaubert, née Comtesse d'Alton-Shée, wife of a high official in the Ministry of Justice and one of the few socialites who remained faithful to the end.

It was at the beginning of January 1848 that Henri Heine paid me one last visit. He had his servant carry him on his back from the carriage up the two flights of stairs to my apartment. The effort made him collapse on the living-room couch, and he was seized by one of those horrible attacks that tormented him to the end of his days: spasms starting in the brain and extending all the way down into the toes. Only morphine could alleviate these unbearable pains. The doctors applied moxas [tufts of a soft, combustible substance for cauterizing] all along the spine; later he once told me that he had come to spend as much as 500 francs a year for this poisonous sedative.

During the attack of which I was the involuntary witness, myself all trembling to see him suffer so much, I could only repeat time and again: What a crazy idea to let himself be dragged about in this state. As soon as the pains seemed to subside somewhat, I implored him to stop all further such excursions until an intelligent treatment had improved his condition.

"My disease is incurable," he replied. "I am going to lie down, and I'll never get up again. I have therefore come, my dear friend, to exact from you the promise that you will come to see me, and that you will never abandon me. And if you won't swear to it, I'll have myself brought back here and will scare you out of your wits once again as I did just now."

Whereupon Henri Heine, all himself again, started to paint a sad and funny picture of the embarrassing situation in which I would have found myself if he had died there on my couch; in the public's mind the fatal event would have immediately been linked to a love affair. "And thus I missed becoming the hero of a charming posthumous novel," he declared, continuing to crack endless jokes without yet losing sight of the promise he wanted to extort. And when, wanting to get him home as soon as possible, I finally gave in, he started all over again. He was proud of his skill at joking about the most depressing subjects and of the way in which he established what he called *le droit de moribondage*, his favorite expression.

THE SPARK THAT set off the revolution of February 1848 in France was a banquet that didn't take place.

Political banquets, an old English custom, had been adopted by the French in the summer of 1847 as a way of voicing and organizing opposition in the face of a ban on mass meetings. The essentially reformist campaign was to culminate in a gala affair celebrating the end of the parliamentary session, to be hosted by the leading citizens of Paris's Twelfth Arrondissement. The Twelfth was a notoriously volatile Left Bank district centered on the Panthéon and including the university, then as now a source of endless trouble for the forces of law and order, which immediately raised strong objections. As a result, the banquet was duly outlawed by a government smugly oblivious to the social tensions in a city of nearly a million inhabitants, one-third of them unemployed, another third working for a pittance and barely able to feed themselves. Yet again it was the students who provided the original cadres in the protest against the ban, and on the morning of Tuesday, February 22—the date of the canceled banquet—some 700 of them marched to the Palais Bourbon, where the Chamber was in session, then crossed the river to the Champs-Elysées, where they were met by an elite company of Dragoons. The soldiers, rather than blocking the student march, reined in their horses and saluted. And by the end of the day, although not much of anything had really happened—one man was killed, some children threw rocks, and a few barricades were thrown up—the reign of Louis Philippe had come to an inglorious end.

The King himself, however, was not aware of it until the

following morning, when the National Guard, on which he had counted to protect him, fraternized instead with the rebels. By midafternoon he had sacked Guizot, his unpopular Prime Minister, but the sacrificial gesture came much too late, the more so since he could find no replacement; no one wanted the job. In the meantime, the people gathered in the streets, and when a column of demonstrators marched on the Ministry of Foreign Affairs, a frightened officer ordered the guards to fire into the crowd. Sixteen men and women died on the spot, hundreds were wounded. It was back to the days of the Bastille and the Spirit of '89.

The corpses were piled on a huge wagon and paraded throughout the night by torchlight all over Paris; by morning a citizen army estimated at well over 100,000 had erected barricades—some 1,512 by the final count—and beat off an attack by forces loyal to the King. After several attempts to form a new cabinet and regain military control of the city, Louis Philippe abdicated on Thursday afternoon, February 24, in favor of his grandson, the nine-year-old Comte de Paris, whose father, the Duc d'Orléans, had been killed six years earlier in a carriage accident.

But at a tumultuous meeting in the Chamber of Deputies invaded by an armed mob, the aristocratic poet Alphonse de Lamartine—of whom George Sand said that he handled all kinds of ideas and all kinds of people without believing a single idea or loving a single creature—proclaimed the end of the monarchy, and the twelve members of the provisional government, appointed by the roar of the crowd rather than chosen by any formal ballot, held their first session at the Hôtel de Ville. By Friday, February 25, the revolution had ended, and France was once again a republic.

•

Heine's condition since the beginning of the year had further deteriorated to the point where on February 6 he, along with Mathilde, her housekeeper-friend Pauline, and the inevitable parrot, settled in a nursing home run by his friend Louis-Grégoire Faultrier. Almost totally paralyzed by then, he obviously required more care than the two women in the house could or would provide, and the hope was that with intensive medical care his state would once again improve to the extent of enabling him at least to attend to his most intimate needs. Aside from Jules Sichel, an Alsatian ophthalmologist whom Heine credited with having saved what remained of his eyesight, his physicians included the long-suffering Leopold Wertheim, a German Jew who once got his face slapped by Mathilde for having criticized her care of her husband, and David Gruby, a Hungarian doctor fashionable among Parisian celebrities. None of them had any idea what ailed their patient, but their very ignorance may have yielded certain therapeutic benefits in that for quite a while it kept alive the hope for eventual improvement, which they passed on to Heine by word and by the mere fact of being willing to undertake some procedure or other. On the other hand, many of their ministrations, such as the standard leeches and the cauterizations of the spine, can only have added to their patient's miseries.

On February 22, as it happened, the night the revolution broke out, Heine had been briefly back in his apartment in the rue de Berlin for a home-cooked meal which Mathilde had prepared for him and Dr. Gruby. At the first sounds of fighting he called for a carriage, but along the way it was stopped by the rioters and used as raw material for a barricade; not until late at night was he able to return to the nursing home.

In the circumstances one can hardly be surprised at his notable lack of enthusiasm for the revolution. But physical discomfort aside, he had other reservations about the change of government—and with good reason, as it turned out. "My feelings about the revolution that took place under my very eyes you can easily imagine," he wrote to Meissner. "You know that I was never a republican and will scarcely be surprised that I have not become one, either. What the world is now striving and hoping for is alien to my heart. I bow to fate, being too weak to defy it, but I am not about to kiss the seam of its dress, not to put it more crudely . . . I would love to escape the to me frightening turmoil of public life for the everlasting spring of poetry and things eternal, if only I could walk again and were not quite so sick." Whether he would have escaped had he been able to seems questionable at the very least. Even confined to the nursing home and cut off from firsthand contact with events outside, he managed to write three articles on the February revolution for the *Augsburger Allgemeine Zeitung*, which he submitted along with a rather desperate postscript to its editor: "Dearest Kolb, I can't see anymore, and I cannot walk two steps. Your poor friend H. Heine." He was still only at the beginning of his martyrdom; such wasteful outbursts of self-pity became rare in later years.

The articles themselves reflect his distance from the center of events, although on the crucial first night luck or misfortune gave him what he called a front-row seat. "The street where I happened to be was blocked at both ends by barricades . . . Which gave me an opportunity to admire the talent for building barricades displayed by the French. Those high bulwarks and fortifications for whose construction German thoroughness would require entire days are here improvised within a matter of minutes . . . The death-defying courage with which the French workers fought should amaze us only in that it arises out of no religious conviction and without any pious hope for a reward in the great beyond . . . And their honesty matched their courage.

[35]

The rich could not get over the fact that the poor, who for three days reigned supreme here in Paris, did not touch anything that did not belong to them. In fact, it struck many people as rather ominous to hear that thieves caught in the act were shot on the spot. With this kind of regime, they thought, no one could ever be sure of his life."

The irony, already rather forced, faded altogether in the two succeeding articles dictated a few days later, still in the nursing home. Their vapid philosophizing reflects the growing despair of a man increasingly cut off from the world and struggling to hear the sound of his own voice, and they end on a quite uncharacteristically flowery note eulogizing Lamartine and the leaders of the provisional government. In the end, the pieces were never published.

But by the time Heine left Faultrier's institution on May 7 and returned to his own apartment, he no doubt had revised his opinions about the new leadership, and his already jaundiced view of revolution may well have soured even further. A sleazy journalist by the name of Taschereau, an early role model for today's investigative reporters, had somehow gained—or more likely been deliberately given—selective access to the archives of the previous regime and made himself a reputation of sorts by entertaining the public with juicy bits of scandal. And one of his discoveries was the existence of a slush fund out of which the former government had secretly subsidized certain prominent writers, among them Henri Heine, who had been drawing an annual pension of 4,800 francs since April of 1840.

The disclosure was more than embarrassing; it seemed to substantiate what so many of Heine's enemies had alleged all along. From within Germany he was being accused of having betrayed his fatherland for a mess of potage, while many of the exiles suspected him of having been paid not so much for writing as for *not* writing about certain subjects the French government preferred to keep out of the public eye. The scandal could not have erupted at a worse time: he was nearly blind and almost totally paralyzed that spring, unable to wield the pen, the one weapon of which he was the undisputed master, while at the same time the paralysis was beginning to affect his jaw as well and made even dictation increasingly difficult. It must have taken an almost superhuman effort for him to defend himself, but he did his best.

In a "Public Declaration" that appeared in the *Augsburger Allgemeine Zeitung* on May 23 he protested the editorial bias with which the paper that had employed him for over twenty years as its Paris correspondent reported the slanderous allegations against him.

The editorial board of the *Allgemeine Zeitung* had ample opportunity over the years to convince itself—not so much on the basis of those of my articles it chose to print as of those it decided *not* to print—that I am not the servile sort of penpusher who lets himself be bribed into silence. It might well have spared me this insult . . . The money I received from the Guizot Ministry was no bribe. It was a subsidy. Or—let us call the baby by its name —it was charity, generously dispensed by the French people to so many thousands of aliens who, by their zeal for the cause of the revolution, compromised themselves more or less gloriously in their homeland and sought asylum on the hospitable soil of France. I accepted these subsidies shortly after passage in Germany of the parliamentary decrees that sought to ruin me, as the leader of the so-called Young Germany movement, by banning not only my existing writings but also all future ones, thus illegally depriving me of all my means of support . . . The reason for the secrecy may well have been the fact that the French government did not want to ostentatiously support a man whose expulsion my royal Prussian friends have been consistently demanding. Mr.

Guizot, however, rejected all such demands and paid me my pension regularly every month, without interruption, and without ever once asking for any services in return. When, shortly after he assumed office I went to see him and expressed my appreciation for the fact that in spite of my radical tint he had agreed to continue my pension, he replied with melancholy kindness: "I am not the sort of man who would refuse a piece of bread to a German poet living in exile." This meeting in November 1840 was the first and last time I ever had the honor to speak with Monsieur Guizot.

It was a valiant if not altogether convincing attempt to disarm his enemies. He came much closer to his real feelings in a letter he wrote a few weeks later to his friend and sometime translator, the Marquis Edouard de Lagrange (whom, in the light of the New Order, he ironically apostrophizes as *Citoyen Marquis*): "I had to swallow a great deal of my pride in order publicly to admit in the *Augsburger Allgemeine Zeitung*, hence before all of Germany, that like all other destitute refugees I asked the French for a handout. And I refrained from pointing out, while making this humiliating confession, that the glory of my name played a major role in the help offered me by the French government, and that France owed a certain measure of gratitude to an author who has consistently fought on her behalf against her detractors on the other side of the Rhine . . . But what will shock you most to know is that this miserable pension was abruptly canceled by one of whom I least expected it—by Monsieur de Lamartine. Yes, Monsieur de Lamartine has canceled the pension of a poor and sick poet named Henri Heine . . . True, I am myself somewhat to blame in that I asked the chief of the accounting department to ask Lamartine to terminate my pension altogether rather than subject it to one of those cuts necessitated by the passions and exigencies of the February revolution. But like so many others, I would of course have gladly made my peace with such a reduction . . . Instead, Monsieur de Lamartine simply struck me from the list of pensioners altogether. I since learned that he thinks I am very wealthy, with an annual income of 25,000 francs."

•

It is doubtful if Heine ever truly grasped the moral ambiguity inherent in this particular situation. He has consistently been portrayed—and not only by his enemies—as a somewhat slippery character of loose morals given to self-aggrandizement, lacking any principles other than self-promotion, and acting as often as not out of sheer opportunism. Most of these charges seem vastly overblown in retrospect, harvest of the dragon teeth he sowed with such generous abandon in the form of barbed comments, polemical attacks, and sarcastic putdowns. He did think of himself as the foremost German poet of his generation, but posterity has clearly validated his judgment on that score. And while his work in both poetry and prose exuberantly defied the pieties and philistine morality of his time, Heine's actual love life appears to have been considerably less extravagant than, with an ostentatious show of discretion, he would have liked his public to believe. In fact, his later domesticity positively shocked many of his free-thinking and free-loving Paris acquaintances (although here the matter of class bias also played a role: to live with an illiterate shopgirl was perfectly acceptable in his circles; to actually marry her was a moral outrage). That his opinions underwent considerable changes in the course of a lifetime is also true, but hardly to be held against him. He was, as has been stressed before, given to questioning rather than faith, and in any case, most of his quarrels with zealots of one stripe or another ultimately came down to personality clashes rather than principles or ideology. But there was one aspect of life in which not only pride but moral as well as ordinary common sense tended to desert him.

Money, of course, often does that to people. Still, the concessions and compromises Heine made for the sake of his finances strike one as weirdly incongruous, all the more so in the light of his insouciant generosity and his well-documented indifference to luxury and ostentation. In later years, of course—the period here under consideration—his medical and mere physical care consumed very substantial amounts even while he was struggling to provide for his widow's future. But his problems with money go back all the way to his earliest youth and clearly have a lot more to do with its symbolic value than with its purchasing power.

Reliable sources about Heine's childhood are simply too skimpy to permit drawing any meaningful conclusions as to the formative influences on his personality. To judge from his letters to her, relations with his mother during the last three decades of his life could best be characterized as condescendingly affectionate. He regularly sent her cheerful, gossipy bulletins that gave no clue as to the state of either his body or his soul; for years he even kept the gravity of his illness from her, until secrecy was no longer possible. Yet she was known as a strong-willed, formidable personality, the daughter of a wealthy physician, herself relatively well educated, and her true role in shaping the character of her firstborn must remain entirely in the realm of speculation, to which certain intriguing references to witch mothers in his later poetry add hints no true psychobiographer would resist trying to interpret. The father, Samson Heine, appears to have been one of those lovable *shlemiels* who, Freud notwithstanding—his own father was another example of the genre—manage to win their sons' unambiguous devotion at the expense of even a semblance of respect. When Samson died in 1828, Heine seemed genuinely heartbroken and grieved for months, even though the foppish little man had never so much as read a single book by his already rather famous son. Moderately prosperous as a trader in English fabrics during Heine's childhood, Samson went bankrupt in 1818 and was bailed out by his brother Salomon, the Hamburg multimillionaire, who not only liquidated Samson's debts along with his business but also had him declared mentally incompetent. Psychologically emasculated, possibly afflicted neurologically as well, Heine's father spent the last ten years of his life in a state of vegetative decline while Uncle Salomon assumed full responsibility for the support of his brother's wife and children, in effect becoming the actual *pater familias* and as such the displaced target of Heine's adolescent rebellion.

Salomon Heine was one of those larger-than-life characters whom it is easy to hate, although his nephew never required any special incentives. In any case, while the uncle gave him ample cause to resent his blunt, imperious ways, Heine's rage in this instance was tempered by awe and a pinch of plain greed he chose to interpret as love. Which it may well have been, for all we know, given the highly elastic definition of this elusive term.

Salomon, originally from Hannover, had parlayed his wife's dowry of 10,000 marks into a fortune of well over 40 million by the time of his death in 1844, proving along the way that being an uneducated, near-illiterate lout is no obstacle to a highly successful career in business and finance and—more important—that even an unconverted Jew could become socially accepted if he had enough money. Salomon not only had more than enough, but in all fairness he also spent much of it on charity, including large-scale relief after the catastrophic conflagration in 1842 as well as the Hamburg Israelite Hospital, which he founded in memory of his wife. He regularly hosted some of the most prominent figures of his time. In one of his letters Heine rhapsodizes about having met the "homerically divine" Field Marshal Blücher, hero of the campaign against Napoleon, at his uncle's dinner table, but he generally felt like the proverbial poor relation he in fact happened to be. Salomon set him up in business, and when, within less than a year, he went bankrupt, Salomon paid for his law studies and more or less regularly contributed to his support until Heine was nearly forty years old. This sort of dependency was bound to foster a profound ambivalence; owing gratitude to a crude vulgarian who had usurped the role of the father but treated the budding genius with humiliating contempt while paying his bills aroused enormous resentment in the beneficiary. Heine's largely unfounded complaints about his uncle's stinginess make sense only in the context of an unconscious displacement that made him feel like a true son rather than a poor relation, to the point where the amount of support—never enough to satisfy him—became a gauge of paternal love. A hypothesis, but one that would explain the vicious, self-destructive fury which for two years all but immobilized Heine both literally and creatively when, after his uncle's death, he was forced to realize that in Salomon's eyes he had been nothing but a poor relation after all, and a naughty one at that; the old man didn't even leave him so much as a keepsake.

Heine's public version of relations between his uncle and himself, however, was that of the eternal conflict between poetic genius and money-grubbing vulgarity, and in the absence of dissenting voices from the other side he had the last word on the subject. Whether he really believed that the world—starting with Salomon Heine—owed him a living because he was a great poet, or whether this in turn was his way of rationalizing needs far beyond the obvious financial ones may be debatable. Not so the fact that in accepting a subsidy from the French government as a tribute to his literary stature he was quite possibly fooling himself but hardly anybody else. The position of a supposedly independent journalist of known radical persuasion being on the secret payroll of a reactionary government is morally indefensible. Heine had no pressing need of the money in 1840, when it was first offered to him. But it flattered his ego, and he accepted it as a tribute to his genius, a token of appreciation, and a bear hug from the notoriously literate French bureaucracy, even though he was far too intelligent not to have known better.

And now, eight years later, disinherited, sick unto death, when he really did need money and could have put those 4,800 francs to very good use, the new government abruptly stopped the pension. And adding considerable insult to the injury, the man who wielded the ax was a fellow poet. Not much of a fellow, and not much of a poet, but still . . .

ON MAY 7, Heine and his retinue left the nursing home and moved back into their apartment on the rue de Berlin. He seemed somewhat improved; he had recovered the use of his hands as well as some sense of taste, and one eyelid remained half open. "A sick man always hopes for better days," he wrote to his publisher. "My head is clear, lucid, even cheerful. The heart, too, is healthy, with zest and craving for life—only the body is paralyzed, wasted."

A few days later he apparently decided to put his partial improvement to the test by visiting the Louvre. "It was in May 1848, the day I left the house for the last outing of my life, that I took leave of the gracious idols whom I had worshipped in times of good fortune," he wrote in 1851, in the postscript to the *Romanzero*. "It was only with the greatest of effort that I managed to drag myself to the Louvre, and I collapsed as I entered the majestic hall, in which our blessed goddess of beauty, our beloved Lady of Milo, stands on her pedestal. For a long time I lay at her feet and wept so vehemently that even a stone would have taken pity. And indeed the goddess looked down at me, full of compassion and at the same time disconsolate, as though wanting to say to me: Don't you see that I have no arms and cannot be of any help to you?"

Caroline Jaubert's version of the same story as he told it to her goes on to quote him: "Why didn't I die right then and there, that very moment? It would have been a poetic death, pagan, superb, the kind I deserved. Yes, I should have perished in this agony." Then, after a moment's silence, switching back into his mocking tone: "But the goddess did not reach out for me. You know what ails her? Her divinity, just as my humanity, is reduced by half. So that, despite all rules of algebra and mathematics, our two halves could not add up to one whole."

The literal truth of the anecdote seems rather beside the point; this was how he saw himself entering the dark night of oblivion, self-mocking, desperate—and fully alive.

Desperate above all, as he finally realized in the spring of '48 that the slight improvement had been merely temporary and that, whatever his doctors chose to say or do, there was no longer any realistic hope of even a partial recovery. It was during those depressing weeks that Fanny Lewald, a prolific German novelist of liberal-feminist persuasion, breezed in to see him, gushing a steady spray of high-minded platitudes which, whatever the patient may have thought of them, struck her as worthy of quoting at length.

Again briefly alluding to his illness [she writes], Heine said: "What most amazes me about this misery is my enormous, my indestructible lust for life. It strikes me as downright spooky. It still haunts the ruins of my self like the ghost of a lovely nun in the walls of a convent."

"Why do you pick such a gruesome image?" I asked. "There was so much life-affirming paganism in you. Why don't you say: I still have so much feeling for nature and life that every ray of sunshine, every human face gives me joy . . . To a pagan like yourself, the gods are bound to grant that joy till the very last breath."

"Never mind the gods," he said. "No pagan gods would have done to a poet what was done to me. Only our old Jehovah would do a thing like that. Even my lips are paralyzed. I can't talk, and I can't kiss."

On May 24, after a mere two weeks in the apartment, he moved to suburban Passy for the summer, "completely paralyzed, so that I can only be in bed or in an armchair; my legs are like cotton, and I have to be carried like a child. The cramps are terrible, and now my right hand is also beginning to die . . . Dictating is painful because of the paralyzed jaw. My blindness at this point is rather the least of my problems."

In spite of which he managed, a week later, to draw up a detailed plan for an 18-volume edition of his collected works, which he sent to Julius Campe, his publisher, with an urgent request to give the matter his immediate consideration. "Danger looms . . . I am a poor and dying man; poor in every respect, with barely enough to cover the expenses of my illness . . . I am in a bad way. What monstrous, miserable bad luck keeps hounding the German poets; may this, too, change in Germany." And as always, he signed his letter "your friend Heinrich Heine."

•

A vast oversimplification; whatever the relationship between Heine and his publisher, friendship in the ordinary sense certainly did not define it. Both sides at one point or another compared it to a stormy marriage, but the emphasis on the purely personal and emotional components misses the context of broader trends that were almost guaranteed to generate permanent tensions between them in their respective roles as publisher versus author, quite apart from the inherently explosive potential of two monumental egos.

Campe, eight years older than Heine, was a giant of a man, obstinate, contemptuous of the authorities with whom he clashed frequently in the courts, but at the same time determined to keep his publishing firm, which he had taken over in 1823, afloat in some very choppy waters. On the one hand, he had to deal with a Byzantine tangle of censorship jurisdictions that required all publications of less than twenty signatures—320 pages—to obtain separate imprimaturs from each German state (the idea being that only scholars and other harmless freaks would read books fatter than that); on the other hand, he had to keep from going bankrupt, which for a publisher of some discriminating taste and political convictions involved a number of painful compromises.

Not an easy balancing act in the best of times, but a real challenge in the Age of Metternich. For more than thirty years, from 1815 to 1848, Clemens Wenzel Nepomuk Lothar Duke von Metternich, Henry Kissinger's role model, had dominated the European political scene through sheer personal brilliance combined with a system of ruthless repression that like the monstrous web of a venomous spider extended all over the Continent and involved entire armies of police spies, torturers, informers, plotters, and liquidators. Rigorous censorship was a key component of this system, with ever more stringent rules and regulations as authors and publishers found ways to circumvent them.

Campe was particularly skilled at this institutionalized cat-and-mouse game; he found so many ways of defying or befuddling the censors that he earned himself a place high on Metternich's enemy list. Campe had one slight advantage in that he conducted his business from Hamburg, an autonomous and relatively liberal city-state not yet part of the German Confederation. But it was Prussia with its 13 million more or less literate inhabitants that constituted the biggest market and also spawned the most scissor-happy censors; any book banned by them was pretty much dead commercially. Campe fought a tenacious lifelong battle against them, partly out of a visceral liberalism and partly out of an innate streak of cussedness; he came up with ever new tricks, such as inserting fake title pages, giving false dates and places of publication, binding innocuous and dissident writings together into one cover. Yet he also lost many a skirmish, and every defeat meant major financial losses. There was a limit to the risks he could afford to take if he wanted to remain solvent, but this was not an argument Heine seemed willing or able to grasp. One of his recurrent complaints about Campe was that the publisher let himself be intimidated much too easily. Which, as Campe finally pointed out to him in a white fury, was a cheap shot, coming from someone sitting in Paris, out of the line of fire.

The other area of constant friction between them, not surprisingly, involved money. A conflict of interest was built into the system from the very start: author and publisher negotiated a fixed amount for the rights to a given work, usually with additional payments due if demand justified further editions. Campe loved his business, he regularly spent 80-hour weeks at it, he took long chances, published most of Germany's dissident writers, and he was not particularly greedy as these things went in his day, but he did want to make money, and he knew how to drive a hard bargain. Heine was a difficult customer who missed deadlines, overestimated his sales appeal, fussed over design and production problems, and denounced any compromise with the authorities. But despite his law degree he proved no match for the entirely self-educated Campe when it came to haggling over the terms and conditions of a contract. It may well be true that the publisher tended to print unusually large first editions so as to avoid repeat fees for subsequent ones. Yet it is also true that the amounts he paid Heine in honoraria and annual pensions were relatively generous, the highest within his own stable and generally on a par with what other publishers paid their top authors. And although Heine sold quite well during his lifetime, Julius Campe's bet did not really pay off until long after both he and his author were gone. In the latter part of the nineteenth century, Heine became Hoffman & Campe's perennial bestseller and made a fortune for his godchild, Julius Campe II; the firm continues to thrive to the present day.

·

None of which can explain or excuse Campe's behavior. At a crucial time in Heine's life, when he needed Campe more desperately than ever before, the publisher simply cut him adrift and withdrew into an inscrutable three-year silence. He conscientiously remitted all payments agreed upon, but from May 1848 to July 1851 this most punctual and long-winded of correspondents did not reply to any of at least a dozen letters from his bedridden author. The reasons for this one-sided breach remain far from clear, and Campe himself never offered more than some vague utterings about having been fed up. A first-time father at fifty-four, he had named Heine the godfather of his son and postponed the christening for two years in the hope that his star author would attend in person. The boy was finally christened in February 1848, with Heine represented by proxy, and there has been speculation that Campe regarded his absence as an insult, the more so since, after being exposed to Heine's constant litany of afflictions over the years, he quite simply refused to credit the seriousness of his condition. In other, less charitable interpretations, Campe emerges as a callow profiteer banking on Heine's imminent demise to raise the value of the property.

Whatever his rationalizations, there can be no excuse for Campe's inhuman cruelty. The true reasons no doubt lie buried deep in the ambiguities of a relationship which, rather than resembling an unhappy marriage, perpetuated long-standing patterns of parent-child dependency, with all their inherent ambivalence on both sides. Campe, with his unerring instinct, was among the first to recognize and bet on Heine's genius, and for a long time he played the by turns indulgent, exasperated, infuriated, or forgiving parent, but how he really felt about the author as a person is far from clear; the fact that he cut his ties with him shortly after becoming at long last a real father in the flesh may or may not offer a clue.

Heine, for his part, dealt with Campe much as he had dealt with Uncle Salomon, both of them father figures whom he constantly tried to goad into loving him; just as he told Salomon that the best thing about him was the name he shared with his nephew, so he truly believed that Campe's greatest asset was his association with Heine. There clearly was more than a dash of jealousy in his contempt for most of the other dissident writers—Börne, Gützkow, Grün, etc.—whom Campe specialized in publishing. He suspected them of conspiring against him, and he ultimately blamed their intrigues for Campe's inexplicable refusal to communicate. It made the rejection somewhat easier to bear.

•

Passy is now part of the Sixteenth Arrondissement, between the Seine and the Bois de Boulogne, but when Heine spent the summer there in 1848 it still had a somewhat rural air about it. At any rate, it was far enough from the center of Paris to spare him the worst of the fighting that shook the city, but his emotional and intellectual distance from events was infinitely greater than the hour's walk that separated him from the Palais Bourbon. His physical deterioration obviously played a very significant part in this detachment, if for no other reason than that it made it impossible for him to gather firsthand information. But his attitude toward the February revolution and subsequent developments had largely been fixed beforehand, anyway, and like most mortals he failed to see what did not fit into his scheme of things.

For the fact was that whatever his distaste for the republic, the new regime had brought about sweeping changes within a remarkably short time—much too sweeping and much too short, as it turned out, but relentless pressure from below drove the agenda of the largely well-intentioned if bumbling intellectuals who made up the provisional government. They established the universal—or at any rate half-universal—franchise, giving every male citizen the right to vote, a right which, in a paradox replayed many times since, doomed democracy within less than a year as the conservative peasant vote swamped the urban liberals. Relief for the unemployed was to be provided by the National Workshops, a work relief program which enrolled 28,000 men in March and a month later had swelled to well over a hundred thousand as the jobless and destitute from all over the country poured into the capital, straining available resources way past their capacity and creating an explosive situation not greatly eased by the free theater tickets the government distributed as part of their drive to raise the general level of culture. Lamartine asked Victor Hugo to accept the Ministry of Education, but Hugo demurred, ostensibly because he did not consider himself a republican. With the abolition of censorship, no fewer than 479 newspapers were started in Paris between February and December, and the official government *Bulletins* were regularly posted every other day through all of France, most of them written by Heine's erstwhile friend and probable lover, the Baronne de Dudevant, alias George Sand. Her passionate republican sentiments had made her rush to Paris from her country home at Nohant at the first news of the revolution; ensconced in the Ministry of the Interior, she took charge of the propaganda machinery and apparently soon realized that the situation was rapidly veering out of control. Tocqueville, in his *Souvenirs*, describes how she gave him "a detailed and singularly lively picture of the state of the workers in Paris, their organization, numbers, arms, preparations, thoughts, feelings and their terrifying determination. I thought the picture exaggerated, but it was not; what followed proved it. She seemed to me pretty frightened herself of a people's triumph and to evince a rather solemn pity for the fate which awaited us."

The first skirmishes took place on May 15, triggered by a parliamentary debate on Poland, a subject dear to the extreme left, which wanted to declare war on Prussia and Russia unless Poland's independence was restored at once. The damage was minimal, but several top leaders of the workers' clubs were arrested, a first step by the right-wing alliance toward forcing a showdown.

The next step was the dissolution of the Workshops, denounced as socialist by the sizable Catholic bloc in the Assembly. Anticipating the inevitable confrontation, the cabinet outlawed the workers' clubs as well as all armed assemblies, to the point where even unknowingly standing next to a person bearing a concealed weapon became a crime. All unemployed nonresidents of Paris were to be given the choice of either joining the army or being shipped back where they came from. On Friday, June 23, the Assembly by a narrow margin defeated a bill calling for the immediate abolition of the Workshops. As a last-minute attempt to delay the inevitable showdown, it was a case of too little and too late. Out in the streets, the barricades were once more going up.

This time around, however, the government's response was swift and deadly, and in General Cavaignac, the Minister of War, it had a brutally effective defender. Aside from regular troops, thousands of national guardsmen were mobilized, and from all over the country peasants, shopkeepers, and *déclassé* aristocrats came streaming into Paris to join the fight against the subhuman proletarians. The insurgents, on the other hand, never numbered more than about 50,000, and their demands were relatively modest— mainly the continuation of the Workshops and release of the imprisoned leaders. But arrayed against them were all the forces of Church and state, backed by fierce class antagonism and overwhelming armed power.

The result was a three-day massacre in which 1,460 people lost their lives, with heinous atrocities committed on both sides. Cavaignac, granted dictatorial powers by the Assembly, declared martial law and a state of siege in Paris that lasted until October, setting a precedent followed later that year by the beleaguered governments in Vienna and Berlin. Of the 15,000 prisoners, some 500 were deported to Algeria, many of the rest were held for over a year; 50,000 troops remained encamped in Paris, their horses eating all the greenery along the Champs-Elysées. The conservative faction had won all along the line and made it the first order of business to repeal most of the social legislation passed in February.

To Marx and Engels, the bloody defeat of the insurgency spelled the death of vestigial illusions and traditional bonds; they believed that it would help to prepare the working class for the imminent final conflict. Alexander Herzen, the great Russian dissident living in exile in Paris, saw it as the death not of illusions but of ideals, the end of hope for liberalism and democracy.

Heine refrained from commenting on the situation, other than reassuring his mother on June 26 that he was all right.

HE WAS, OF COURSE, far from all right.

He was totally paralyzed from the chest down, he was more than half blind, he was married to a woman who neither could nor would take care of him, who was unable to so much as read the newspaper to him, so that for even the most mundane services he had to rely on hired help or the kindness of friends. His first nurse, a pretty young woman to whom he became attached, was fired for that very reason by the ever-jealous Mathilde and replaced with an ogre, dubbed by him *la Vieille Garde* (a pun referring to Napoleon's elite guard), whose ministrations he came to dread. Campe not only failed to respond to his letters but also ignored his plea to remit all payments due him in cash rather than in bank drafts, "because I can no longer leave the house, cannot even get up from my chair, and therefore have to conduct all my business by mail."

He was still given to bouts of self-pity and not yet fully adept at the icy self-control, the flippancy, and the gallows humor with which he later attracted and entertained his visitors, sole lifeline to the outside world, sparing them the need to grapple with their horror, pity, and shame and ultimately helping him, in turn, to triumph over his own despair. The summer of '48, his days and nights in Passy must have been among the most terrible in Heine's life— on the one hand, the definite end to any hope of recovery, the realization that he would spend what remained of his life imprisoned in a near-dead body, and on the other, the sense of a world come off its hinges, his impotence at what even out in his suburban retreat he sensed to be a crucial moment in history. As it turned out, the shape of the future was about to be decided for at least a century to come, and in his instinctive, impressionistic way Heine saw it more clearly than most of the self-anointed prophets of his age.

In August, in a letter to Jean-Jacques Dubochet, a Paris publisher who distributed Hoffmann & Campe publications in France, he complained bitterly about being

nailed to a mattress while everyone is on his feet and everything is moving. The news from my country exacerbates my torments. At this precise moment, when I should have been more active than ever carrying on my work of a lifetime, I am condemned to paralysis, unable even to respond to the cries of distress of my friends, who plead with me for the help I always used to give them in the past. Our enemies have gotten the upper hand in Germany. The so-called national parties, the Teutomaniacs, are strutting about with an insolence as ridiculous as it is brutal; their boastful rantings are beyond belief. They think the time has come for them to assume the leading role on the stage of world history and to bring their lost tribes east and west back into the fold, and if you don't hand Alsace back to them in a hurry, they'll demand the Lorraine along with it, and God only knows how far their teutomaniacal ambitions are going to take them. War is what they want, and in this they are of one mind with our princes, whom nothing would please better than to channel the bellicose ardor and fighting spirit of their rebellious subjects into a foreign war. I've received sad news from beyond the Rhine: France's most devoted friends, who spent twenty years trying to dismantle Prussian power in the Rhineland provinces, no longer dare fight against the rise of nationalism and have hoisted the flag of the German empire.

•

It seems rather doubtful if Heine, even at the height of his powers, could in any way have influenced the course of German history.

[55]

The German worship of Order, Organization, and Obedience amounts to a form of national genius which, whatever its stellar achievements—Auschwitz among them—seems to make effective rebellion inordinately difficult and successful revolution all but impossible. What defeated the liberal and progressive forces in 1848–49 was not only the firepower of the Prussian Army but the spirit of its founder, the flute-playing, homosexual philosopher-martinet Frederick II—chest out, belly in, trap shut. The second major upheaval in German history, the revolution of 1918, was led by men who, with tears in their eyes, apologized to the Kaiser for having to depose him. And finally, the army conspiracy against Hitler in 1944, prepared with pedantic attention to every detail, so much so that when the key component—Hitler's assassination—failed on the first try, the whole plot simply collapsed because none of the high-level conspirators seemed capable of taking independent action on the spur of the moment, a lack of initiative bred into them and for which they paid with their lives. In a sardonic poem entitled "1649–1789–???" composed around this time in one of his sleepless nights, Heine, in fact, proved uncannily prophetic. After citing the executions of Charles I and Louis XVI, the final stanza envisages a similar revolution in Germany:

> *Französen und Briten sind von Natur*
> *Ganz ohne Gemüt; Gemüt hat nur*
> *Der Deutsche, er wird gemütlich bleiben*
> *Sogar im terroristischen Treiben*
> *Der Deutsche wird die Majestät*
> *Behandeln stets mit Pietät.*
> *In einer sechsspännigen Hofkarosse,*
> *Schwarz panaschiert und beflort die Rosse,*
> *Hoch auf dem Bock mit der Trauerpeitsche*

*Der weinende Kutscher—so wird der deutsche*
*Monarch einst nach dem Richtplatz kutschiert*
*Und untertänigst guilloniert.*

*(The French and the British by nature are wholly devoid of feel-*
*ings. Only the Germans have feelings; they will remain complai-*
*sant even while exercising terror. The Germans will always treat*
*Their Majesties with all due reverence. It is in a black-draped*
*coach with six horses driven by a weeping coachman that the*
*German monarch will someday be taken to the place of execution*
*and guillotined with pious reverence.)*

He was wrong about the guillotine, but he certainly caught the spirit of the so-called revolution of November 1918 some seventy years before it took place.

The situation in 1848 was exceedingly complex, involving as it did not only a triangular class struggle—aristocracy, bourgeoisie, and a nascent proletariat—but also the last-ditch battle between Protestant Prussia to the east and the far more liberal western regions, centered on Frankfurt am Main as the capital of the German confederation. It lent itself to hopeless ideological confusion and regional conflicts, but by the end of 1849 the uprisings throughout the country had been crushed, the defeated rebels were hunted down and massacred by the hundreds, and the silent majority of see-no-evil citizens opted for order—which in Germany has always taken precedence over law—and a rabid nationalism championing unification under Prussian rule.

Germany, it can fairly be said, never quite recovered from the catastrophic defeat of liberalism in 1848—although, in a rare gesture of magnanimity, the victorious Prussian King granted his repentant peons the right henceforth to smoke in Berlin's Tiergarten, the municipal park. The defeat effectively aborted the moderating political influence of the rising middle class before it had ever properly begun to make itself felt, and it poisoned the intellectual atmosphere for at least a century; between 1848 and 1945, Germany and Austria were the only countries in the Western world where students formed the vanguard of nationalist and later Fascist reaction, and where faculties were dominated by right-wing extremists.

But it was in Vienna and in Budapest that the bloodiest, the most promising, and the most tragic of the 1848 uprisings took place. For nearly six months, a unique alliance of students and workers ruled Vienna, banished Metternich, proclaimed freedom of the press, introduced a host of liberal measures, and at the end of October was beaten by an army of Croatian mercenaries. After reconquering Vienna, the imperial armies moved against revolutionary Budapest, which under the leadership of Lajos Kossuth had declared Hungary's independence. They took Budapest on January 4, 1849, killed hundreds of resistance fighters, and raised anti-Semitism to an official policy, leveling a heavy fine upon the entire Jewish community. But the Hungarians regrouped and in short order beat the Austrian regular troops; by midsummer, the entire country was back in their hands. At this point, a desperate Austrian Emperor appealed for help to the Russian Czar, and in an eerie preview of events in our own century, a Russian army of 140,000 men defeated the Hungarians in August 1849, even while the Hungarians vainly pleaded for American and British intervention. After an orgy of mass slaughter and a prolonged reign of terror by the Austrians, the Imperial Hapsburgs stumbled onward into a morass of sloth, stupidity, and absolutism that made even the Metternich regime seem liberal in retrospect and whose disastrous long-range effects are still to this day being played out in all of Eastern Europe. Kossuth himself escaped to Turkey and was brought to the

United States, where he received a hero's welcome and collected funds for an army of liberation that never got off the ground. Among the victims was Sandor Petőfi, one of Hungary's greatest poets, killed at the age of twenty-six in the Battle of Segesvár, just when the first German translation of his selected poems was being published. The translator dedicated it to Heinrich Heine.

•

Heine's reactions to these momentous events were on the whole rather subdued. He was not a political animal and hardly qualified as an objective observer, but when he went beyond sarcastic comment and relied instead on his true gut feelings, he could be remarkably astute—not infrequently rather in spite of himself. To the end of his days he never failed to stress his status and vocation as a *German poet*; it was to be the epitaph on his tombstone, and in both poetry and prose he immortalized the hopeless longing of the exile for the fatherland. Yet insofar as he had a spiritual home, it was the language rather than the land, with its harvest of bigotry and repression, and a distinctly false note often creeps into his lyrical affirmations of nostalgia; whatever his "dreams of Germany in the night," in broad daylight they tended to turn into nightmares. He was and remained an outsider, incapable of the effusive chauvinism so stridently proclaimed even by the majority of his fellow émigrés in Paris. Which greatly accentuated his isolation but gave him an insight into the nature of German nationalism that proved deadly realistic.

•

On September 19 Heine returned to Paris. "I don't want to be buried in Passy; the cemetery there has got to be real boring. I want to move closer to the one on Montmartre, which I chose long ago as my final place of residence." Well-meaning friends urged him to move south to the then still unspoiled Riviera, but he scoffed at the idea. "What air, no matter how balmy, what region, no matter how delightful, what earthly paradise could take the place of this pestiferous fog that makes me cough? . . . A truly spirited human being can live and die only in Paris. The air, I admit, is polluted, the pace is too fast, but you are in an intellectual atmosphere that penetrates the most distant and lonely of places. The life of the entire universe is concentrated in Paris. Don't talk to me about Nice and other southern delights. Let me die right here. The exile would kill me down there much quicker than the illness up here. Never take a goldfish out of the filthy water of its aquarium, any more than Heinrich Heine out of the Paris air."

Rather than moving back to the rue de Berlin, Heine settled at 50, rue d'Amsterdam, in the Ninth Arrondissement, a dark, depressing place that figures prominently in the memoirs of many of his visitors and where he was to spend the next six years of his life. Located on the second floor, in the rear of a six-story building, his apartment had a hall, kitchen, living room, dining room, bedroom, and toilet, one regular and one servants' entrance as well as a garret on the sixth floor for the help. The main attraction seems to have been the rent, inordinately cheap at 700 francs a year, but with five or six people and one screeching parrot sharing this limited space, privacy and silence were at a premium. Heine required a nurse in attendance or at least available around the clock, as well as the part-time services of a secretary; Mathilde, in addition to a cook, had her housekeeper-companion Pauline, from whom she was inseparable.

Even an able-bodied human being of moderate sensitivity would have been under considerable strain in these circumstances; Heine inexplicably—even to himself—seems to have settled into them with well-nigh saintly serenity.

His physical sufferings, from the disabling headaches and gruesome spastic contractions to the medieval tortures that passed for treatment, may have made the stresses of a cramped, noisy household seem comparatively benign, and the opium on which he increasingly came to rely, either orally or in poultices applied to a neck wound deliberately kept open, undoubtedly also had a soothing effect. But from the tone of his letters and the testimony of eyewitnesses it appears evident that by the end of 1848 he had undergone a spiritual transformation of sorts. Faced with the choice between futile rage and a resigned acceptance of his fate, he had opted for the latter.

Inevitably, this conspicuous newfound serenity aroused a great deal of curiosity and gave rise to rumors about another repentant sinner's return to God. Conversions *in extremis*, at a time when fear and desperation numb the brain, seem to provide a peculiar satisfaction to those committed to the notion of a Supreme Judge swayed by deathbed repentance, and Heine had a number of visitors eager to encourage him in what seemed to them his belated search for divine mercy. One of them, the Princess Belgiojoso, a close friend and political exile who in the 1840s returned to Catholicism and went on a pilgrimage to the Holy Land, mistook Heine's keen interest in her trip for a religious awakening and persuaded him to receive the Abbé Caron, a priest noted at the time for some sensational conversions among Parisian intellectuals. After three visits, however, Heine declared that as far as comfort and consolation went, he preferred poultices to religion: "They act more quickly."

And in a letter of September '48 to Caroline Jaubert: "The spasms, far from improving, now involve the entire spine and rise all the way up to the brain, where they may perhaps have done more damage than I suspected; religious ideas are bubbling up."

This is not to deny Heine's spiritual quest in the face of death, a quest which at this stage had only just begun. But as in so many other ways, he defied the conventional schemes of ideology and religiosity ultimately to find, or at least to come close to, fulfillment in the one realm he could claim as uniquely his own.

AFTER THE JUNE UPRISING in Paris with its several thousand victims—among them the Paris archbishop, Monsignor Affre, who had attempted to negotiate a peaceful surrender—General Cavaignac in effect ran the country as a dictatorship pending the ratification of the new constitution on November 12, 1848. It called for a strong executive, the main dispute centering on the method for electing the President. A sizable faction wanted the choice to be made by the Assembly, which unquestionably would have elected Cavaignac. But Lamartine, the spiritual father of the Second Republic and fatuously certain of his own popular appeal, insisted that it be determined by popular vote and, for the last time, won his point.

In the election, held on December 10, he obtained all of 8,000 votes; 38,000 went to the leftist militant Raspail; 370,000 to Ledru Rollin, the champion of universal suffrage; 1,450,000 to General Cavaignac. But 5.5 million voters, about 75 percent of the electorate, cast their vote for a man who had grown up in exile in Switzerland, been kept out of France until the beginning of the year, and been practically unknown even a few weeks before the election but whose name set every true French heart aflutter with nostalgia: Louis-Napoléon, nephew of the late lamented and unforgotten Empéreur.

He spoke French with a strong German accent, behaved circumspectly, took no firm stance on any issue so as to avoid antagonizing any faction, and was considered much too stupid to present a threat to either the republic or any of its dominant politicians, the less so since under the provisions of the new constitution he was elected for only a single four-year term and could not succeed himself.

As it turned out, the ostensible stupidity was part of an elaborate act, and Louis-Napoléon eventually revealed himself as a superlative actor who successfully deceived everyone around him. For several years he contrived to conceal utter ruthlessness and unbridled ambition behind a mask of simpleminded bonhomie, all the while cunningly plotting the coup d'état that would restore him to what he considered his rightful place as his uncle's legitimate heir. An Englishman who met him at the time recalls: "I did not expect to see so utterly insignificant a man, and badly dressed into the bargain . . . When Prince Louis-Napoléon held out his hand and I looked into his face, I felt almost tempted to put him down as an opium eater. Ten minutes afterwards I felt convinced . . . that he himself was the drug, and that everyone with whom he came in contact was bound to yield to its influence." And his own cousin, Prince Napoléon, said about him that "he never says anything and he always lies. He is such a liar that you can't even believe the opposite of what he says."

As a lifelong admirer of the uncle, Heine was originally pleased with the emergence of what seemed to be a level-headed and innocuous young member of the clan. And if he lacked glamour, the name itself more than made up for the missing charisma; the adulation of Napoleon Bonaparte was by no means confined to the French alone. His initially victorious armies carried the message of the French Revolution across the Rhine and into Central Europe, among the most immediate beneficiaries of *égalité* being the Jews, who, throughout the areas occupied by the French, for the first time enjoyed full rights of citizenship. Moreover, in Heine's native Düsseldorf, the local population seems to have enjoyed particularly cordial relations with the army of occupation. French soldiers practically became part of the household during Heine's childhood, and the subsequent liberation by the Prussians was far from being universally appreciated.

Heine himself always freely acknowledged his emperor worship. What he did not talk about and quite possibly never let himself realize was the extent to which it isolated him in early adolescence and stoked his hatred of Prusso-German chauvinism. He was twelve years old when Napoleon's army suffered its disastrous defeat in Russia. A year later, in the fall of 1813, an anti-French alliance defeated Napoleon in the Battle of Leipzig, and on March 31, 1814, he was forced to abdicate as Prussian troops entered Paris.

This so-called War of Liberation and Prussia's leading role in it, suitably enhanced and reverently garnished with tales of legendary heroism, became one of the fundaments of neo-Teutonic mythology. It spawned a superpatriotic frenzy that raged with particular virulence during the years immediately following the war, which happened to coincide with Heine's late adolescence, and despite the awed account of his dining with the warrior idol Blücher at Uncle Salomon's home, it is not easy to imagine him sharing the effusive chauvinism of his peers, whose heroes proceeded to restore the divine rights of the Prussian Junkers while his own hero was on his way to Elba.

Actually, most German Jews should have shared his misgivings as the victorious Prussians hastened to dismantle the essentially progressive legislation introduced by the French and, among other retrograde moves, revived the severe legal discriminations against the Jews. The fact that many, perhaps most of them, not only swallowed their disappointment but emulated the superpatriotism of their gentile compatriots testifies to an amazing capacity for self-deception, whose tragic denouement we came to witness in our own century. Heine at least partially transcended this particular conflict of loyalties by escaping into romantic poetry; he had his first major success at twenty-one. But it would be strange if these dissonant experiences, coupled with the sharp rise in overt anti-Semitism during his student years (in 1822, Jews were excluded from all academic posts in Prussia), did not permanently color his views of his fatherland and its natives.

As for Louis-Napoléon, the later Emperor Napoléon III, Heine concluded in 1852 that he had turned out to be a lion disguised in the skin of an ass, rather than the other way around, as was the rule with politicians generally. Despite, as he put it, a lingering case of sentimental Bonapartism, he was outraged by the coup d'état and foresaw trouble. By the time it came, Heine was dead; and in the end the lion turned out to be an ass after all.

•

A famous anecdote told by Alfred Meissner casts a strange light not only on Heine, Mathilde, and their marriage, but also on Meissner himself.

During the winter of 1849 he was an almost daily visitor, on whom Heine came to rely for newspapers and outside news, as well as literate and literary gossip in his own language. Mathilde for her part constantly complained to Meissner about the insulting behavior of "those Germans" who came tramping in day and night demanding to see Henri and about the lack of respect with which they treated her. Meissner finally felt obliged to set her straight and put an end to her complaints:

"You cannot draw conclusions about the character of an entire nation on the basis of some dozen or so writers who happen to be living here," I told her . . . "Moreover, you unwittingly paid the

Germans a great compliment by praising Seuffert as the only German who, in stark contrast to the others, displays the qualities of an impeccable gentleman. Seuffert, you see, happens to be the only true Teutonic German out of the entire crowd. All the others are also, well, yes, German citizens, but not real Germans. They are Jews. The Jews have lived among us for centuries and yet there are certain characteristics, both good and bad, that persist and that distinguish them."

Flabbergasted, Mathilde cried out: "Jews? I know about Alexander Weill. He told me himself that he once wanted to become a rabbi. But what about the others—Jeiteles, for instance? The name sounds so arch-German."

"I think I can assure you that our friend Jeiteles is not of Teutonic origin."

"Then what about Abeles and Bamberg?"

"The same."

"Oh no, you're wrong," Mathilde cried out triumphantly. "They can't be Jewish. It's not possible. Do you mean to tell me that Kohn is a Jew? Kohn is related to Henri, and after all, Henri is a Protestant."

I suddenly shut up. Like a man crossing a frozen lake and suddenly seeing a crack in the ice, I realized that I was on treacherous ground. Quite by accident I had come upon the seemingly unbelievable fact that Heine had never told his wife about his origins and that she, naïve as she was, knew nothing about them.

Heine himself on a number of occasions confirmed that Mathilde was ignorant of his Jewish origins and that he had done nothing to enlighten her. Whatever his motives—fear of rejection, a realistic grasp of her very limited intellectual capacity—they reveal glimpses of a relationship between an indulgent older man of the world and a capricious, none too bright little girl that bears scant resemblance to a marriage between adults. And in fact it started out in 1834 as a conventional affair between a sugar daddy and a *grisette*; he married her seven years later, on the eve of a potentially fatal duel, intent on legalizing the union out of concern for her future. This concern, touchingly paternal, not only persisted but proliferated throughout his illness, to the point where even on his very deathbed it still inspired desperate efforts on his part to provide for what he wished or needed to see as an aging, spreading, and perennially helpless child. In his letters and conversations he invariably professed an uxorious passion so ardent as to render it suspect on sight, and many of his friends entertained grave doubts about the ostensibly idyllic nature of the marriage and about the childlike naïveté of what to a great many outsiders looked like a tough, cantankerous, and shamelessly egotistical woman.

Then again, many of his friends were snobs or "Germans," and the fact remains that Mathilde stuck with the invalid till the end. Till almost the end, that is. Quite possibly she saw in him little more than a meal ticket, a rather generous one at that; there is every reason to believe that she accounts for many of the perennial cash-flow problems that dogged Heine in spite of a relatively good income. On the other hand, she may have been genuinely fond of him in her own way, though she definitely fussed a great deal more about a sick parrot than about a sick husband.

At any rate, to say that intellectually these two disparate creatures had nothing in common would be a gross understatement. Barely literate in French, Mathilde never read a line of Heine's work and had no idea of his standing in the world. She summed up her impression of him in an oft-quoted verdict: *"Henri, c'est un très bon garçon, très bon enfant; mais quant à l'esprit, il n'en a pas beaucoup."*

All of which leaves Heine's abiding devotion to her something of a puzzle. The sexually provocative teenage mistress in time became the chubby child-wife, child rather than wife, and cherished as such for reasons having to do with Heine's own emotional underdevelopment. He fled intimacy in whatever form, be it in friendship or in love, and certainly could not have sustained a lasting relationship with intellectual equals such as George Sand or the Princess Belgiojoso. Which still fails to explain why he remained as parentally fond of Mathilde as he did, why he put up with her tantrums and incessantly worried about her widowhood. It seems psychologically simplistic yet much more in line with the available evidence to suggest—as a number of his contemporaries suspected—that the dread scourge of Prussian censors, philistines, and kings was an inordinately decent and tenderhearted human underneath the bluster, notoriously fond of children and haunted by a sense of responsibility for the one creature he had vainly sought to transform, Pygmalion-like, from Crescence into Mathilde —from *grisette* into *Hausfrau*—leaving her dangling between worlds.

•

One may give Meissner the benefit of the doubt and assume that the sententious hectoring he quotes as his own contribution to the exchange with Mathilde was simply a later stylistic adornment. Nevertheless, the implications of his remarks, which he obviously saw no reason to disown even as he wrote them down, are intriguing insofar as they come from a relatively open-minded and progressive German liberal. Your visitors, he in effect tells Mathilde, behave badly because they are Jews. They have lived among us Germans for centuries, but in some ways they still aren't quite civilized. Not like us.

It is an unwitting, hence all the more convincing, example of the attitude toward Jews which prevailed throughout the nineteenth century among all too many Germans who proudly considered themselves unbiased and liberal.

•

One of the "Germans" of whom Mathilde evidently disapproved happened to be Dr. Leopold Wertheim, a refugee physician who combined a solid medical background with the sort of humane approach in which most of his colleagues seem to have been sadly deficient. He was almost the only doctor in whom Heine had full confidence, so that it came as a rude shock when Mathilde, furious because of some critical remark of Wertheim's about the way she took care of her husband, threw a fit and blackened the doctor's eye; he thereupon refused to ever again set foot in the house.

You have no idea [Heine pleaded with him in a letter a few weeks later] how often and how intensely I think of you every day, how every occasion reminds me of your compassionate friendship, and how vast a void has opened up within me ever since you withdrew. Until now I did not have a German-speaking secretary, otherwise I would have told you right away how much suffering the incident has caused me. It stems from the same source of misery that has already precipitated so much bitterness, i.e., *the madness* of a beloved being, which erupts every so often and is as unaccountable as it is incurable. There is no use complaining or trying to change things; one has to suffer and forgive with patience and forbearance. But for me personally it is the greatest of misfortunes not to be able to see you anymore and not to have anyone with whom to talk freely about everything that troubles me, physically as well as mentally . . . I feel a little less close to death and actually sit upright in a chair every day for half an hour or so, but my condition depresses me more and more, though I keep quiet about it.

It speaks for Dr. Wertheim that he eventually relented and let himself be persuaded to again take charge of Heine's care.

[70]

In the course of the year, his condition had steadily deteriorated, as he informed his brother Max, the self-ennobled physician at the court of St. Petersburg:

I still suffer day and night from the most horrible cramps. They now involve the abdomen and the chest, and since I can only lie on my side in a fetal position, my digestion has also become increasingly difficult and I often have to torture myself inhumanly for a couple of weeks before I have a movement. The only means of relief is morphine; I sometimes take as much as seven grains in twenty-four hours and live in a savage stupor. How is this going to end? . . . Just the same, I have lately written some poems . . . trying to divert my spirit from melancholia into other regions, yet even this resource will soon dry up because the combination of pain, facial spasms, and opiates is bound to empty the head . . . Since I myself am no longer able to retaliate for the evil people do unto me, I have turned the entire business of liquidating my life over to God.

Whatever the effect of the opiates on his digestion, they not only failed to "empty his head" but in the long run proved the only medicine worthy of the name. More than a medicine; "May no one say that I lack religion," he at one point quipped, "opium, too, is a religion." There is no question that without the unrestricted availability of opium and its derivatives, liberally prescribed and taken in huge and ever-increasing doses, he would not have lasted nearly as long as he did. And, more important to both him and the world, the work of his final years would have been unthinkable.

Already in April of 1849 he announced to the still pouting and silent Campe that he spent a great deal of his time composing verses, and that some of them had the strange power to relieve his pains when he repeated them to himself over and over like magical incantations. Few of these, products usually of sleepless nights, survived the rigorous screening process he applied to all his work and for which he relied, had to rely, on his one eye, halfway serviceable as long as he propped up the lid with the thumb and index finger of his left hand. His imagination was primarily visual, to the point where he found it impossible to finish a poem to his satisfaction unless he first saw the written word on the page, a need he himself ascribed to the "plastic nature" of German. "Our language is made as much for the eye as for the ear, and in verse the writing is as decisive as the sound." Every artist is entitled to his pet theory.

His virtual entombment notwithstanding, he managed until almost the end to do some scribbling in his own hand, in foot-high letters, propped up on his side and, as he put it, with his nose practically touching the paper on the low table by his bedside. But the regular routine was for him to wait for the arrival of morning and his secretary, to dictate the creative harvest of the night and then discover, on examining it in the cold light of day, that there were few pearls among the lot worth preserving. Karl Hillebrand, in later life a well-known author and historian, fled to Paris in 1849 at the age of twenty, after having taken part in the uprising in the state of Baden, and served as Heine's secretary from October 1849 until he was expelled from Paris in the summer of 1850. Though he refused to divulge any intimate details about the Heine household as "a violation of their trust in me," he recalls that

it took morphine in three different forms for him just to get some peace, usually no more than four hours of sleep. And it was in those sleepless nights that he composed his most marvelous poems. He dictated the entire *Romanzero* to me. The poem was always ready in the morning, but then began the polishing, which took hours . . . Every present and past tense was probed and weighed, every obsolete or unusual word questioned, every superfluous adjective cut out . . . He also dictated private letters, usually having to do with money matters. The rest of my daily visit of about three to four hours was devoted to my reading to him. The scholarly books I have long since forgotten, because they did not interest me and I just read them off more or less mechanically. For the most part they dealt with theology or church history . . . as well as the Bible, which he knew almost by heart and out of which I often had to read him whole chapters, mainly in the Old Testament. Newspapers didn't much interest him, at most the *Journal des Débats* once in a while . . . But we read a great number of poets . . .

As I said, I do not wish to divulge any personal details, but I must stress that Heine always treated me with a kindness and loving consideration that have left deep traces in my heart. Nor did he forget me when, in the summer of 1850, I was forced to leave Paris. He insisted on helping me out with what little he had, and it was only with the greatest of effort that I eventually prevailed upon him to let me repay the loan which he wanted me to keep as supplementary wages.

THE PRICKLY AGGRESSION with which Heine
shielded a complex and vulnerable inner self from the ever-
present threats of ridicule or intimacy began to change. The
ever-increasing demands on his psychic and physical ener-
gies left less and less room for elaborate posturings; survival
in what he called his mattress tomb—the mattress a miserable pallet and the tomb his own dying body—required
a relentless focusing of whatever strength he had left. What
he discovered was that the weapons he had always wielded
to keep the world at bay would serve him just as well in
his struggle against himself—against the howling despair,
venomous self-pity, and other deaths-in-life. The grim gallows humor and flashes of irony with which he entertained
visitors and correspondents to make them forget, if even
only for a moment, the horrors of his slow dying were no
longer lex of an inwardly lonely child in Düsseldorf, and
although the protective carapace evolved over the years
from brash defiance to more or less subtle irony, the vast
discrepancy between who he was and who he appeared to
be persisted. Only the work itself offered occasionally lu-
minous if fleeting glimpses of a man patently at odds with
the perennial devil's advocate he played with such consummate wit.

But with his physical collapse, the game of defensive
showmanship became as much an act of self-control, indistinguishable from gallantry. It cannot have been easy to
preserve some scraps of dignity in the face of near-
continuous pain, and even the routine of daily care was a
steady, humiliating assault on his sense of self. But when,

in the presence of visitors, the aging mulatto nurse carried this lifeless bag of bones about as if he were a rag doll, he urged them to "be sure and tell the world that the Parisians carry me on their hands." Increasingly he was becoming the person he had always chosen to impersonate. And just as for him day and night had lost their meaning and fused into a timeless blur, the gradual resolution of so many of the inner conflicts and contradictions lent new depth to his vision. The poetry that surfaced was unlike anything he had written before. It is unclear just when, after his total degeneration, he first found the strength to resume work, but all through the year of 1850 he defied the miseries of body and soul and kept on writing. He wrote in order to live. He went on living in order to write. Given the harrowing circumstances under which he was forced to labor, there is no way of telling how much he actually produced as against what he eventually chose to preserve. But he published nothing in the course of that year, with the exception of *In October 1849*, a powerful and bitter lament over the defeat of liberty in Germany and in Hungary, which circulated as a pamphlet and suggests that he was still alive to the world after all:

*Gelegt hat sich der starke Wind,*
*Und wieder stille wird's daheime;*
*Germania, das grosse Kind,*
*Erfreut sich wieder seiner Weihnachtsbäume.*

*Wir treiben jetzt Familienglück—*
*Was höher lockt, das ist von Übel—*
*Die Friedensschwalbe kehrt zurück,*
*Die einst genistet in des Hauses Giebel.*

*Gemütlich ruhen Wald und Fluss,*
*Von sanftem Mondlich übergossen,*

*Nur manchmal knallt's—Ist das ein Schuss?—*
*Es ist vielleicht ein Freund, den man erschossen . . .*

*(The storm has settled, quiet has returned. Germania, big baby,*
*again enjoys her Christmas trees. We're promoting family hap-*
*piness now; any higher aims are pure evil. The peaceful swallow*
*is back nesting under the gable. Woods and rivers are cozy and*
*quiet, bathed in soft moonlight. Except that now and then there*
*is a loud bang—was that a gun? A friend, perhaps, whom they*
*have shot . . .)*

But in the end, after venting his rage over the massacres
in Vienna and in Hungary, his own helplessness is starkly
brought home to him:

*Das heult und bellt und grunzt—ich kann*
*Ertragen kaum den Duft der Sieger.*
*Doch still, Poet, das greift dich an—*
*Du bist so krank, und schweigen wäre klüger.*

*(There's all that howling, grunting, barking, and I can't abide the*
*stench of the victors. But hush, Poet, this will do you no good—*
*You are so sick, and silence would be wiser.)*

It was the only poem he permitted to circulate; all the
others he hoarded for what, in a letter to Campe, he announced as "the third pillar of my lyrical glory"—after the
*Book of Songs* and the *New Poems*—"carved out of the
same, if not an even better strain of marble."

•

Need and greed can be a spur to creativity; they can also
cripple the artist. The financial difficulties with which
Heine, on top of all his other problems, wrestled during

the last decade of his life have elicited a great deal of commiseration, nor was he ever reluctant to feel eloquently sorry for himself on that score. All of which tends to obfuscate the rather significant gap that existed here, too, between the reality of Heine's situation and his perception of it. The reality was that, as has already been noted, he had a relatively good income and that, even in his final years, when the illness necessitated large additional outlays, he was never in any serious trouble. It goes without saying that the gang of philistine multimillionaires whom he honored by being a member of the family could, without noticeable strain on their purses, have granted him a life and death free of such petty concerns instead of treating him like a shiftless welfare recipient. Still, they would hardly have let him starve—if for no other reason than the bad publicity—and neither would his friends, who included the Baron de Rothschild and, most particularly, his wife, Betty, an ardent fan of Heine's writings. That he was plagued by frequent acute crises is true, but these may have had more to do with Mathilde's extravagance and her shortcomings as a housekeeper than with anything approaching real poverty.

He worried endlessly about money. "It is already expensive enough to *live* in Paris," he wrote Campe in November 1849. "But dying in Paris is infinitely more expensive. And to think that I could now be hanged for free in Germany or in Hungary." Yet as long as he dealt with money as a mere medium of exchange, a means of putting bread on the table, hiring a secretary, paying the doctor, buying opium, and keeping Mathilde happily occupied shopping and cruising the boulevards, it confronted him with realistic problems that did not eat into his soul's innards and, on the contrary, may have given him an additional incentive to focus on his work. He played the stock market, investing

[77]

mainly in railroad shares, and had some modest gains, thanks in part to James de Rothschild's market tips and occasional gifts; yet as we saw in relation to the crash of '47, even losses sustained in the normal course of events left him reasonably unfazed. It was when money came to stand for something far beyond its own intrinsic value and assumed a much broader symbolic significance that Heine could not deal with it in any manner approaching rationality. The most glaring example, of course, was the already mentioned "inheritance feud," the failure of his millionaire uncle to leave him a pension or any other token of his affection. After raging and ranting for a year, enlisting countless intermediaries, organizing elaborate plots, and threatening his cousin's family with scandalous revelations, he ultimately caved in. For the sake of a miserly pension, Germany's greatest poet, exiled for his refusal to submit to the power of state censorship, agreed to publish nothing derogatory about Carl Heine and his appendages and allowed this singularly dense and bigoted halfwit to exercise a *de facto* censorship over his writings. Whether or not Heine, as a result, actually destroyed major parts of his *Memoirs*, as he claimed, is open to some doubt; if indeed they existed, they were more likely either seized after his death by Carl Heine or sold to him by Mathilde. But in any case, his craven surrender to unvarnished blackmail seems difficult to reconcile both with his self-image of unbending pride and with the arrogant assertiveness of the public persona. And while the money undoubtedly came in handy, no objective need can quite explain such extremes of self-inflicted humiliation.

Some of the same childishness—there is no other word for it—characterized his behavior in another financial affair, with somewhat similar emotional overtones, which preoccupied him for much of 1850. And in both instances the same brilliant but deeply flawed Mephistophelian figure played a key role in triggering what at times verged on lunacy.

•

Ferdinand Lassalle, born in 1825, the son of a Jewish businessman from Breslau, was one of the most flamboyant and charismatic political activists among the rebellious young German intellectuals. A powerful orator and facile writer, he was the rising star of the socialist movement, long in an uneasy and rivalrous relationship with Marx until he founded his own labor party in 1863, while at the same time conspiring with Bismarck against the liberal center. But for all his genuine gifts—there are those who believe that he might have become a German Disraeli—Lassalle was doomed as a politician by serious character flaws that ultimately cost him his very life. Vain, preening, temperamental, impatient, quick to wax passionate and just as quick to lose interest, he proved unable to establish any solid footing in either politics or the world of ideas. Moreover, he perennially let himself be distracted by side issues that engaged his fleeting passion or his quixotic sense of justice; thus his first great cause, which brought him to the attention of the public at large, was a lurid eight-year court battle in which, with the aid of incriminating evidence purloined from his opponent, he won a favorable divorce settlement for a socially prominent countess. His last great cause was a hopeless love affair with the daughter of a Prussian diplomat, whose fiancé killed him in a duel in August 1864. He was thirty-nine years old. A meteor rather than a star, after all.

One of Lassalle's early causes happened to be Heine's feud with his family, and there is little doubt that his intervention helped to make matters considerably worse. The two met for the first time in 1845, and Heine, not given to facile enthusiasm when it came to people, was apparently swept off his feet.

He was barely nineteen when he first came here [he later wrote to his brother Gustav] and never has a young man made a greater impression on me, both by his knowledge and by his personality. What especially struck me was his quick turn of mind and the sort of energy in which my own dreamy character is so sadly deficient . . . I also was in a highly excitable mood at the time because of the Salomon inheritance affair and my anger at the family. And no one grasped more clearly than Lassalle just where the shoe pinched me, which is to say that money matters were not really the main issue and that my rage had to do with much deeper and older wounds, wounds I neither could nor would bare in public. No need to tell you about them, either, though you cannot possibly imagine how despicably I have been duped and defrauded by people from whom I least deserved such treatment and who had no need for it . . . This whole miserable affair was driving me crazy, and at that precise point I met Lassalle. His passionate nature was both helpful and harmful; he poured oil on the fire and goaded me into making all sorts of wrong moves . . . But this man in his rapid evolution toward evil has become one of the most sinister of scoundrels, capable of any crime, from theft and forgery to murder, while at the same time endowed with an intense single-mindedness bordering on insanity. I don't want to have anything to do with him.

As usual in Heine's case, things were a touch more complicated than he chose to present them. The groundwork for this *coup de foudre* had been prepared by Heine's long and worshipful friendship with Lassalle's sister Friederike, three years older than her brother, uncommonly attractive but inconveniently married to a speculator by the name of Friedland, whose fortunes were subject to wild fluctuations.

In 1846, briefly prosperous, Friedland persuaded Heine to invest 12,500 francs in a company planning to introduce gaslight into Prague. Like most writers, Heine had no real understanding of the workings of capitalism; he adored Friederike and was smitten with Lassalle at the time, reason enough for him to trust the speculator, whose promise to triple the investment in short order did not set any bells ringing.

When it eventually became clear that the Prague gas company dealt mostly in hot air and was headed for bankruptcy, an indignant Heine demanded his money back. The thought that investment involved risk had apparently never occurred to him, but over and above the actual loss, it was the sense of a trust betrayed by those whom he had considered his friends that so outraged him. He launched a campaign of threats against Friedland, implicated Lassalle, appealed to Lassalle's father, and had some of his German and Austrian contacts publish polemical pieces denouncing the criminal conspiracy to defraud a poor and helpless poet. For months he raved and ranted, until at last Friedland, hounded and compromised, meekly surrendered and agreed to repay the money in installments as soon as he was able to.

•

Poetry, financial worries, gossip, polemics, and a host of daily aggravations kept him distracted up to a point. In September Pauline Rogue, household factotum and Mathilde's constant companion, became seriously ill, so that for the ensuing four months two bedridden patients had to share whatever space, care, and comfort were available in the small apartment. Visitors still came to pay homage or to satisfy their curiosity, though Heine complained about his increasing isolation. "I see few Germans, except for passing strangers. Meissner was here, and I saw much of him . . . Seuffert had eased up on the drinking and embraced religion, but now he seems to have combined the two and added love in the bargain; Bacchus, Christ, and Amor constitute his latest Holy Trinity . . . I've lost and mourned my friend Balzac [who had died on August 18, 1840]. George Sand, the bitch, has not been heard from ever since I've become ill; this great emancipator of women, or perhaps I should say emancimator, has done an outrageous injustice to my poor friend Chopin in a most repulsive but divinely written novel. I am losing one friend after another."

But the progress of his illness was unrelenting and undeniable, and even his stoicism, his unflagging sense of humor, and his quiet, almost secretive concentration on his work could not quite banish the shadows. In March he informed Dr. Wertheim that "only morphine still gives me some relief. My condition is so tragic that even I am beginning to feel sorry for myself, which my inveterate ebullience had thus far kept me from doing. I don't take any more medications; neither doctor nor pharmacist can help me." And in a letter to Heinrich Laube, a young German writer and friend, Heine speaks of the "despair of the body" even while momentarily succumbing to the despair of the soul: "You cannot imagine how much pain I have to suffer . . . with no hope for improvement, and the depressing near-certainty that these torments may well grow much more horrible still toward the end." Adolph Stahr, Fanny Lewald's husband, who passed through Paris in October, reports a conversation in which Heine compared his own conditions with that of his friend, the historian Augustin Thierry—"who is completely blind, bedridden just the way I am, and unable even to move his arms. The fact that I can still do this is what keeps me going, because it assures me my freedom of action. Whatever I suffer I put up with because I can still bear it—and because I can put an end to it whenever I feel like it. You see, with this hand I can still reach a dose of opium on the table that would put me to sleep forever, and next to it there is a dagger which I still have the strength to use if the pains become unendurable. Having this final freedom is what gives me courage and, so to speak, cheers me up."

On the other hand, there is the testimony of Caroline Jaubert, who on one of her visits noticed a curious contraption with ropes and a kind of stirrups fastened to the wall above his head. "A gymnastic invention," he explained, "supposedly to help me exercise my right arm. But frankly, between you and me, I rather suspect it to be an invitation for me to hang myself, a delicate hint from my doctor. But you know," he went on, "there are idiots who admire my courage to go on living. Have they ever figured out a way for me to kill myself? I can neither hang myself nor poison myself, let alone blow my brains out or jump out the window. Which means I'd have to let myself starve to death, and that is against all my principles. Seriously, one either should at least be able to choose the manner of killing oneself or else forget about it."

Both versions sound more or less authentic, and in any case, consistency was never one of Heine's hobgoblins.

WHETHER AND TO WHAT extent Heine in adversity sought the comfort of religion is an open question whose answer pretty much depends on the ideological commitments of the questioner. Those convinced that "there are no atheists in foxholes" will discern in his references to a personal God an affirmation of their beliefs, whereas unrepentant atheists and agnostics are likely to dismiss his scattered invocations of divinity as little more than elaborate sighs. Or curses. "Thank God I now have a God again, so that when the pain gets too bad, I can let go of a few blasphemous curses. Atheists don't have that satisfaction."

Early in 1850, highly sensationalized reports began to circulate in the German press about the prodigal son's repentance and return to God. Whether pure invention or based on some of Heine's notoriously ambiguous remarks as understood by certain visitors is irrelevant; the tale of the sinner who denies God, is punished for his sins and led by the mortification of the flesh to seek the mercy of the Lord gave self-righteous newspaper readers in the age of syphilis every bit as much satisfaction as it still does in the age of AIDS. In a letter to his mother in January, Heine simply denounced the stories of his so-called conversion as the usual pack of lies, but writing to his friend Laube a few days later, he was more specific:

Much of the current gossip about my newfound faith and piety is one part nonsense and two parts malice. No great changes have taken place in my attitude toward religion, and the sole inner upheaval I can report to you with certainty and self-assurance is a sort of February revolution in my thoughts and views about religion. In place of the previous principles, which left me rather indifferent, I now have adopted new ones, which also don't engage me fanatically and have certainly not made for any sudden fundamental changes in my feelings. In other words, I have abandoned Hegel's god, or rather Hegel's godlessness, and reverted to the dogma of a real, personal God external to nature and the human mind . . . Hegel has greatly dropped in value with me, and old man Moses is flourishing.

This seems to me one of the most persuasive assessments of Heine's attitude toward religion, a rare instance of an objective self-portrayal on his part. His relationship to Hegel, one of his teachers at the University of Berlin, underwent several sea changes, but at no point was it ever that of an unconditional, let alone fanatical disciple; Heine was constitutionally incapable of being either a follower or a leader. With Moses, on the other hand, despite a lack of personal acquaintance, he was on a much more intimate footing, though here again his qualified sympathy fell far short of outright worship. Throughout much of his life he professed to adore the Greeks and their gods, one reason among many why he so strongly identified with Byron in his youth. In his philosophical essays he contrasted the Greek love of life with the asceticism of what he chose to call the spirit of the Nazarenes—"that morbid little sect that gave birth to Christianity and the Christians"—and from the retrospective of his mattress tomb, at any rate, he looked back on his youthful self as a joyful Hellene, a sort of laurel-crowned child of the gods cavorting among the earthbound mortals. It was an image he may have attempted to project, but it seems doubtful if he ever convinced anyone, least of all himself; Heine—unlike Byron, some of whose works he translated and whom he referred to as his spiritual cousin—for all his often effusive romanticism never quite lost sight of reality. In his heart of hearts he never took the Greek gods any more seriously than he did Jehovah, except that the latter was a presence familiar since childhood, and one whom during those endless, sleepless nights he no doubt found it far easier to talk to than to those cantankerous louts on Mount Olympus.

There is ample evidence that, child not of any Greek gods but of the Enlightenment, he was himself rather embarrassed by this "religious upheaval . . . more an act of reason than an emotional transformation." But he read a great deal in the Bible, and Meissner reports a conversation from the summer of 1850 that sounds thoroughly authentic: "If I could only walk with crutches," Heine said to me, "do you know where I'd go?" "No idea," I said. "Straight to church."

"You're joking," I exclaimed, in disbelief. "Not at all. Straight to church," he said. "And where else would you go on crutches? Now if I could walk without crutches, that would be a different matter. I'd cruise the boulevards and visit the Bal Mabille."

Nevertheless, many friends of his younger years who had themselves found their way back to God read about his conversion and felt impelled to express their gratification. In October, Adolph Stahr brought and read to him a letter from Karl August Varnhagen von Emse, a Prussian diplomat of rather atypically progressive views, husband of Rahel née Levin, hostess of Berlin's most famous salon; the obvious conjunction between his views and his marriage had forced his retirement in 1824. Rahel, one of the first to recognize Heine's talent, died in 1833, but the widower, increasingly lachrymose and pietistic but politically unreconstructed, remained in touch with Heine till the end and consistently supported him in all his battles. The letter, Stahr reports, took Heine's spiritual rebirth for granted: "Your sufferings, dear Heine, are among my own most painful experiences. You, of all people, did not deserve this. Yet we are forced to deal not only with God but with people as well. How happy we'd be if we only had to deal with Him, for He is all mercy, love, compassion." "Heine laughed out loud," according to Stahr. " 'That sly old fox,' he exclaimed. 'How does he know that?' "

The irreverence was basic to his character, yet at the same time he obviously went to great lengths to reassure his friends and himself that he had not become a religious nut but merely found a personally more satisfying belief system. Whether he really did depends on how one defines belief, hardly a matter of great moment as long as it served its purpose. "When they sprinkle a little of that gray powder into those horrible wounds they burned into my back and the pain stops right away, isn't that the same calming power inherent in religion? There is more of a kinship between opium and religion than most people realize. You see, I have the Bible, I read much in it; rather, I have someone read it to me. A marvelous book, this Book of Books. But when I can no longer bear my pain, I take morphine. If I can't kill my enemies, I leave them to Providence, and when I am no longer able to take care of my affairs, I hand them over to God. Except for financial matters; those I still like to handle myself."

Finally, there is his letter to Georg Weerth, the satirist and literary associate of Marx, written after the publication of the *Romanzero* in November 1851: "I am glad you liked my preface. Unfortunately I had neither the time nor the inclination to express what I had intended to do; that is to say, I am dying as a poet who needs neither religion nor philosophy and wants nothing to do with either. The poet understands both the symbolic idiom of religion and the abstract obfuscations of philosophy very well, but neither the Lords of religion nor of philosophy will ever understand the poet."

•

Much more convincing than Heine's discovery of a personal God was the reaffirmation of his Jewish roots, about which he clearly felt a great deal less defensive. When, in January 1850, one of his German visitors hesitantly alluded to the fact that according to rumors circulating back home he had "returned" to Judaism, he vehemently protested. "I am not returning to Judaism, because I never left it."

Which in one sense was true enough.

He was technically a convert to Protestantism. But, in fact, the reluctant baptism of Harry Heine at Heiligenstadt on June 28, 1825, born again as Christian Johann Heinrich Heine, was a farce, and treated by him from the very beginning as a meaningless concession to practical necessity; in the wake of the post-Napoleonic reaction, most positions in Prussia were closed to unbaptized Jews. Already half a year later, in December 1825, he warned his friend Moses Moser against following his example. "I would indeed feel very sorry if you viewed my own baptism in a favorable light. I assure you that if the law permitted me to steal silver spoons, I would never have converted." Nor did it save him from anti-Semitic attacks by literary critics. "Isn't it crazy—the moment I am baptized, they attack me as a Jew. Altogether, I have had nothing but trouble ever since."

A more pertinent question, however, concerns the nature of the Judaism that Heine insisted he had never left. First, of course, the childhood memories of a Jewish household which, while far from Orthodox, probably still observed certain Jewish holidays and customs. (He was never explicit on the subject.) He briefly attended a Hebrew school run by a distant relative, where he presumably was exposed to a few Bible tales and the Hebrew alphabet, but there is no evidence of his ever having had a bar mitzvah. On the other hand, he received his elementary education in a French Catholic school, an indication of the extent to which indifference if not tolerance toward religious allegiance prevailed in the Düsseldorf of his childhood. It turned out to be a very temporary state of affairs, at least as far as the Jews were concerned, but he apparently did not come up against open anti-Semitism until his student days, beginning in 1819.

This happened to be a critical period in German-Jewish relations, and Heine in many ways personifies the dilemma. Progressive thought, rooted in the Enlightenment, strongly favored the emancipation of the Jews, while at the same time condemning Judaism itself as a retrograde and separatist cult. Baptism in the circumstances became more than a meal ticket; it generally constituted the critical first step toward expunging all vestiges of Jewish identity altogether, the price of admission to a Western society that at the time still mistook itself for civilized.

The extent to which Heine was atypical in this respect has seldom been duly appreciated. He was, in fact, remarkably free of any complexes about his Jewish origins and never hesitated to affirm them, most defiantly so in the face of the anti-Semitic trends that increasingly came to infest German nationalism in the wake of the Prussian victory over Napoleon. But during his student years he nonetheless still believed in the possibility of a true German-Jewish symbiosis, the idea that Jews could become true Germans and be accepted as such without ceasing to be Jews. It was an illusion shared by many young Jewish intellectuals of his time, committed on the one hand to the struggle for civil rights as the way to genuine equality and, on the other, to rendering the Jewish heritage meaningful to their own generation. In 1819 a number of them founded the Verein für Kultur und Wissenschaft—Society for Culture and Science—in Berlin, dedicated to the preservation of that heritage within the larger framework of modern science, the emerging universal creed of mankind. The essentially irreconcilable conflict between these disparate goals became obvious in short order as the Verein struggled to rescue landmarks of Jewish thought while at the same time providing a basic education for lower-class urban Jews, and it collapsed under the weight of internal contradictions in 1824. But for several years Heine volunteered time as an instructor and became closely associated with the leading lights of the movement, his clear-eyed view of the mission's illusory nature more than outweighing the erudition of his associates. Their scholarly monographs on highly esoteric topics of the most limited interest, which Heine criticized as fatuously unreadable, constituted about the only lasting result of the society's efforts; but Heine's involvement and his close contact with men like Leopold Zunz, later an eminent Jewish historian, and Eduard Gans, a moving spirit of the Verein who abruptly converted for the sake of an academic chair, greatly helped a still unformed young man to orient if not to find himself and gave him a valuable grounding in Jewish history. When Gans, after his conversion—which took place shortly after Heine's own—began publicly to extol Christianity, Heine's comment was that "if he means it, he is merely being stupid; if he does it out of hypocrisy, he is a scoundrel." Evidently he soon realized that Gans, whatever his shortcomings, was far from stupid and decided to dedicate a poem to him entitled "To an Apostate," which, thanks to history's notoriously circular motion, figures among his most quoted and quotable lines:

*Und du bist zu Kreuz gekrochen,*
*Zu dem Kreuz, das du verachtest,*

*Das du noch vor wenig Wochen*
*In den Staub zu treten dachtest!*

*Oh, das tut das viele Lesen*
*Jener Schlegel, Haller, Burke—*
*Gestern noch ein Held gewesen,*
*Ist man heute schon ein Schurke.*

*(You groveled before the cross, the very cross that a mere few*
*weeks ago you wanted to trample into the dust. It's the books that*
*do it; reading too much Schlegel, Haller, Burke. Only yesterday*
*a hero, today a treacherous rogue.)*

There are many passages in Heine's work over the years
testifying to his unswerving allegiance to a Jewish identity,
whatever he understood by that. One striking example was
his red-hot fury at the passivity of French Jewry when, in
1840, the French consul in Damascus publicly supported
accusations of ritual murder against a number of Syrian
Jews, who, after being tortured, "confessed" to the crime.
"The French Jews have been emancipated far too long for
the tribal bonds not to have been loosened," he thundered
in one of his articles for the *Augsburger Neue Zeitung*.
"With them, as with the French, gold is their daily god and
industry the prevailing religion . . . Their interest in the
Damascus affair amounts to a few trivial manifestations."

Tribal solidarity never kept him from castigating Jews
when he thought they deserved it, and some of his cari-
catures were cruel in the extreme. But he never indulged
in the kind of obsessive Jew-baiting common among many
other apostates of the day, such as his enemy Ludwig Börne,
né Leb Baruch, or his friend Karl Marx, grandson of Rabbi
Meier Halevy Marx, who made a habit of spewing anti-
Semitic epithets with an abandon bordering on pathological
self-hatred. Heine, like most mortals, may on occasion have

had reasons for hating himself, but having been born a Jew was not among them.

Whether, on the other hand, his tribal allegiance provided comfort in the long night of his dying remains a secret between him and Jehovah, with whom he seems to have had a discreet, somewhat contentious, but rather intimate one-on-one relationship.

ONE OF HIS MORE perceptive visitors noted that in contrast to most agnostics who, no matter how radical their politics, turn strictly orthodox the moment they have health problems and obey their doctors to the letter, Heine retained his thorough skepticism also in matters of medicine. "My sole comfort is that my mind has remained lucid. I consider this so essential that I made a point of keeping mentally busy throughout my illness, even though the doctors consider it harmful. I believe the opposite is true; I think it helped to keep my condition from growing worse. I have never felt any harmful effects from strenuous thought; on the contrary, it cheered me up."

He told his mother in March 1851 that he had used no medications at all for the past two years and that Mathilde had chased all doctors to hell, "with the exception of a single one [Dr. Cruby], who is so tiny that I can almost say he doesn't count. One should always choose the least of all evils. Nevertheless, I don't think I'll ever get back on my feet again. I have finished with this life, and if I didn't suffer too much from constipation here on earth and were sure to receive a reasonably good reception in heaven, I would patiently put up with my existence." At the same time he studied the standard textbooks dealing with his illness—or what he thought of as such—with the zeal of the true hypochondriac, though again with few illusions as to their practical usefulness. "My researches," he declared, "are not likely to help me very much. At best I'll be able to lecture in heaven on how ignorant the physicians on earth are when it comes to treating spinal degeneration." But it is true nonetheless that in the end he himself was the one who hit upon what was probably the most effective therapy available at the time. "There are," he said, "two ways of conquering severe pain—opium, and work." He availed himself of both remedies, and in downright heroic dosages.

·

He had been turning out poems throughout much of 1850; by the beginning of the new year he was ready to think of publication. Campe still refused to answer his letters, other publishers beckoned, and a savvy though not altogether reputable literary entrepreneur suggested a subscription scheme that struck Heine as tantamount to begging. "If I have to beg, I'd want to do it with a loaded gun in my pocket; I'd find that less humiliating. I'd rather you came up with something that amounted to mugging or arson, but please, no subscription lists."

Yet Campe, despite his stubborn silence, continued scrupulously to honor his contractual obligations, and Heine was afraid to make any move likely to jeopardize the semiannual payments he had regularly been receiving from him. He suspected that the publisher, not counting on any further manuscripts, had simply been waiting for him to die so as to exploit the usual brief spurt of interest that follows an author's death and to publish a collected edition with minimal expense in royalties and no interference from an ever-nitpicking poet. Heine was probably right about Campe's motives, but refused to draw the obvious conclusions about his character; whatever the nature of the transference, he continued to treat him as a friend and quite accurately predicted that the man would come running the moment he found out that there was still another bargain to be had. On April 21, he fired off a missive which, though still addressed to "Dearest Campe," for the first time dripped with vitriol. After acknowledging receipt of the semiannual payment of 600 marks, he informed him that, since he was still waiting for the courtesy of a reply to his previous letters, he had nothing further to say.

Except for this: my thanks for the books you sent me, or at least for the goodwill you thereby demonstrated. So these are the radiant blossoms of creativity you bred and cultivated in the last few years . . . the immortal monuments to German thought whose publication consumed so much of your money that you were forced to ignore my many appeals for help and support in my hour of need. You should be complimented on your truly great sacrifice on behalf of humanity, for by sending the money that all those books cost you to me instead, you could have acted in merely your own self-interest. It would have involved no risk, since I was always in your power, and you would now have a sure claim to a manuscript whose popularity, as I intimated, should rival that of the *Book of Songs* . . . I was entitled to expect this help from you, instead of which you chose to wrap yourself in silence. But I am now about to receive generous help from another party, which should prove more useful to me than anything I could have expected from you. I find it impossible to understand how from the very beginning you could have so grievously abused my goodwill, my concern for your interests, I'd almost say my stupid devotion and affection. But there is no point in discussing it any further, since the future is beyond remedy and I already have one foot in the grave.

Campe's reaction was swift, and exactly as Heine had anticipated; he arrived in Paris on July 19, and five days later the two of them signed a contract for a collection of poems for which Campe chose the title of *Romanzero* and for which without much haggling he offered to pay a total of 6,000 marks, or 12,000 francs, for its day a very substantial amount and higher than any he had ever agreed to. To ascribe his relative generosity to a case of bad conscience may be crediting him with more sensitivity than he possessed. But to one who for years had been made to listen to Heine's complaints about his health and been convinced that he once again vastly exaggerated his sufferings, the appearance of this skeletal paralytic must have come as a rude shock and may have stirred some retrospective misgivings about that three-year sulk. In any event, character is not among the vital ingredients necessary to a great publisher; what he does need is a flair for recognizing genius and for presenting it to the public. And there is no doubt that Campe qualified on all counts.

He was enthusiastic about the *Romanzero* and threw himself into producing it with his customary energy and with a speed that could never be matched in this day of electronic publishing; the contract was signed on July 24, and the book appeared about two months later, at the end of September. Even more remarkable is the fact that the end product of this concentrated frenzy turned out not only to be a masterpiece of book production but also marked a bold innovation that seems to have been Campe's own idea and represented a lasting contribution to the book trade: Heine's *Romanzero* was the first book ever to feature a dust jacket.

But as usual in such situations, everything that could go wrong did so and, along with the self-imposed tight schedule, put Heine under enormous stress. He had originally intended to include his *Doktor Faust* as part of the book, but Campe objected on the grounds that the ballet's "obscenities" would greatly reduce the *Romanzero*'s sales potential among female readers, and it was decided instead to bring it out simultaneously as a separate volume. This left the *Romanzero* somewhat short and forced Heine to come up with eleven more poems on very short notice.

Campe in turn tried to stretch out the text by printing the third section with four rather than five four-line stanzas to the page, which prompted furious protests from Heine, ever sensitive about the appearance of his creative progeny:

It is I, not you, who have to defend the book intellectually before the public, and the dreadful impression created by this typographical dissonance damages me morally. I cannot permit this, and no matter how sick I actually happen to be, I'll do my utmost to produce an adequate number of pages without your having to resort to a kind of typographical lockjaw . . . In the meantime, it has got too dark here for me to be able to read today's proofs. Poor devil that I am, I thought I had reached the end of my troubles; now I realize that I am still only in the midst of them . . But with every new book I always want to appear neatly dressed before my readers, with no buttons missing; that four-stanza page of yours makes me so to speak lose my pants in public.

Letters, proofs, and corrections shuttled back and forth between Hamburg and Paris on a daily basis, delivered with a speed and reliability that went out of fashion along with the steam-driven locomotive and the horse-drawn mail coach. Despite his severely limited eyesight, Heine insisted on going over every page. He furnished several additional poems and extended the preface, which ultimately became the epilogue in the published version, and he was certainly more than justified in calling the end result a veritable miracle, given his physical condition. Yet the excitement and the commotion also provided him once more with a sense of being alive and part of the action.

•

Personally he considered the *Romanzero* weaker than his previous books and looked forward to its critical reception with some apprehension, which reached a high level of anxiety as Campe geared up for a publicity campaign that would have made any other author salivate. He commissioned a jacket design for both the *Romanzero* and the *Faust* from an exceptionally gifted young artist and Heine admirer and, in his own hand, wrote to several hundred booksellers all over Germany promoting the forthcoming publication. "The way my publisher keeps pushing the book is bound to generate a reaction against me even if I were a Homer or a Shakespeare," Heine complained. He turned out to be right, although the reaction had ultimately more to do with the contents of the book itself than with Campe's advertising campaign, which initially proved hugely successful. The *Romanzero* went through four printings within the first four months, including a gilt-edged luxury edition, with a sensational total of 21,000 copies in print by the time it ran out of steam and the tide began to turn. The book was banned in both Austria and Prussia, hostile reviews appeared, and sales slowed down to a point where eight years were to pass before a new edition became necessary. Still, Campe had ample reason to be satisfied with the return on his investment.

Heine's unique mastery of the German language and the way in which he transformed it into a medium of his own idiosyncratic expression more than legitimizes his claim to being a *German poet*, in spite of the many reservations and qualifications with which this self-definition must be hedged. At the same time, this very mastery raises a host of problems. Thus any attempt to convey the essence of his work to an audience with no access to the original is soon bound to run up against an insuperable handicap: the bulk of it is quite simply untranslatable. This, needless to say, applies mainly to the poetry, but even the ironic undertones, barbed sarcasm, and sometimes grossly unfunny humor of the prose have seldom been successfully rendered into another language.

The French have come closest, in part of course because Heine was able actively to contribute but also because among his translators there happened to be one Gérard Labrunie, alias Gérard de Nerval, himself a poet of genius. Heine said of Nerval that "he was pure soul rather than man, the soul of an angel . . . who, without knowing much German, was able to grasp the essence of a German poem better than those who had studied the language all their lives." At the time, however, he was a desperately poor, lonely, and lovestruck young man whose own writings attracted scant attention and who, after his first breakdown in 1841 at the age of thirty-three, was in and out of mental institutions until his suicide in 1855. And yet Nerval, among all of Heine's Paris friends, was probably the only one with whom he experienced a measure of genuine emotional kinship.

The first English translation of Heine's complete works by Edgar Alfred Bowring appeared in 1858, only two years after the poet's death. It was a less than inspired effort, followed in 1904 by the much improved version by Leland, Brooksbank, and Armour. In 1911, John Payne perpetrated a rather disastrous three-volume clunker of a translation, and finally Hal Draper's twenty-five-year labor of love, a modern English verse translation of Heine's complete poems based on the standard German edition, was published in 1982. It is far and away the best of the lot. The poems rhyme, and the reader innocent of German can get a fair idea of what they are about. But ultimately neither Hal Draper nor Louis Untermeyer, whose translations of Heine's selected poems are probably the model in the field, can persuade me that it is really possible to convey the essence of what constituted Heine's genius in any language but his own—which is probably as remote from that of Chancellor Kohl as it was from Metternich and Bismarck.

This much by way of a warning to anyone not able to read Heine in the original. Secondhand critical opinions about the work are inevitably subjective and usually biased.

•

The *Romanzero*, divided into three artistically somewhat uneven parts, marks a decisive advance over all of Heine's previous writings and contains some of his greatest poems. At the same time, it also reflects the circumstances of both its creation and its production—the physical agony, the emotional strain, as well as the pressures imposed by unrealistic deadlines and the need to fill blank space so as to avoid "typographical lockjaw."

This is particularly noticeable in the epilogue, which is uncharacteristically rambling despite some labored attempts at self-irony. Heine speaks of himself as being imprisoned in "a tomb without repose, death without the privileges of the dead, who are not required to spend money or write letters, let alone books—a sad state of affairs. They took my measure long ago for the coffin and for the obituary, but in the meantime I am dying so slowly that it is getting boring for myself as well as for my friends. But have patience, there is an end to everything. One of these mornings you'll find the booth closed where the puppet show of my humor so often entertained you."

The first part of the book under the heading "Histories" justifies to some extent the choice of the overall title, shrewdly chosen by Campe to exploit Heine's still lingering reputation as a romantic poet. And the "Histories," in fact long narrative ballads about heroes, kings, and poets doomed in one way or another by destiny conspiring to defeat greatness and elevate villainy, do not on the whole seem radically different from much of what Heine had been writing in the past—stories told with almost vernacular ease, laced with sudden flashes of wry humor and sardonic asides. The section, which opens on a light note with two quite genuinely funny poems, ends on a grim one, a ballad about the defeat of the trusting Aztecs by the treacherous conquistadors and the vengeance the Aztec god Vitzliputzli threatens to wreak upon the Europeans.

It is in the second part, with its bibical title of "Lamentations" that a new and much darker voice makes itself heard. The long narrative ballads have a harder edge, the satire is stinging, but the true lament of both poet and man breaks out in the twenty powerful short poems subtitled "Lazarus" with which the section ends—bitter, morbid, nasty, and all of them reverberating with the basic questions that those of little faith never tire of asking: Why does the supposedly Almighty permit evil to prevail in the world? And why does He pick on me, of all people?

The next-to-the last poem, "Last Will and Testament," with its echoes of François Villon rather than Job, offers some idea of the prevailing spirit

Nun mein Leben geht zu End',
Mach ich auch mein Testament;
Christlich will ich drin bedenken
Meine Feinde mit Geschenken.

Diese würd'gen, tugendfesten
Widersacher sollen erben
All mein Siechtum und Verderben,
Meine sämtlichen Gebresten.

Ich vermach euch die Koliken,
Die den Bauch wie Zangen zwicken,
Harnbeschwerden, die perfiden
Preussischen Hämorrhoiden.

*Meine Krämpfe sollt ihr haben,*
*Speichelfluss und Gliederzucken,*
*Knochendarre in dem Rucken,*
*Lauter schöne Gottesgaben.*

*Kodizill zu dem Vermächtnis:*
*In Vergessenheit versenken*
*Soll der Herr eu'r Angedenken*
*Er vertilge eu'r Gedächtnis.*

*(Now that my life is nearing its end, I am making my Last Will and Testament. Like a good Christian I wish to offer the following presents to my enemies: These worthy, virtuous adversaries shall inherit all my sickness and my misery, all my aches and pains. I bequeath unto you the abdominal colics that grip the belly like a pair of pliers, the bladder troubles and the miserable Prussian hemorrhoids. You shall have my cramps, my bloody spittle, twitching limbs, and spinal rot, all of them God's own great gifts to man. And by way of a codicil: May the Lord doom you to oblivion when you're gone and wipe out all memory of you.)*

The third section, with a bow to Byron, is entitled "Hebrew Melodies." It consists of three long poems that deal in some rather roundabout ways with Heine's exceedingly complex and ambivalent feelings about his Jewish heritage. The first, "Princess Sabbath," describes with on the whole rather gentle irony and even a touch of real sentiment the metamorphosis of the ordinary poor and harried workaday Jew into a Sabbath prince relishing his *Schalet, schöner Götterfunken,* "which is what Schiller would have written had he ever tasted this divine dish." The second and more ambitious by far is "Jehuda ben Halevy," in which Heine's abiding fascination with the Jewish aristocracy of medieval Spain and his view of poetic genius as a divine gift on at least a par with mere royalty merge in a powerful poem loosely focusing on the Sephardic poet Yehuda Halevy. Heine claimed that it was never really finished, but the fragment of almost nine hundred lines that he did leave us certainly stands on its own and qualifies as one of the more important of his creations. "Disputation," on the other hand, the final poem of the *Romanzero*, is among his best known—a debate in medieval Spain between a rabbi and a monk on the fine points of theology which, in real life, usually ended with the immolation of the Jew as an act of Christian charity. Heine's account, peppered with crude jokes about such sacred topics as circumcision, the Holy Trinity, and Jewish dietary law, is a savage anticlerical satire in which both men, working themselves into a sweat, appear equally biased, fanatic, and ridiculous. In the words of the French Queen, asked to judge the relative merits of the opponents and their arguments:

> *Welcher recht hat, weiss ich nicht—*
> *Doch es will mich schier bedünken,*
> *Dass der Rabbi und der Mönch,*
> *Dass sie alle beide stinken.*


*(I don't know which one is right, but it seems to me that as between the rabbi and the friar, both of them stink.)*

Which should put Heine's "return to the fold" into a nuanced perspective.

The *Romanzero* was a book which, despite many understandable weaknesses, turns out in retrospect to have sounded the first notes of an entirely new kind of poetry, and it seems hardly surprising that the German public of its day soon turned against it. Ironically it was in France, a country he loved in his way but whose poetry he did not even think worthy of a sneer, that Heine's influence as an innovator first made itself felt. The *Romanzero* came out in Paris in 1852 in an excellent translation by Saint-René Taillandier and received a generally warm reception. Some of its poems may well have spoken to the *poètes maudits*, but at the time of Heine's death Verlaine was only twelve years old and Rimbaud barely two, while Baudelaire was to bring out *Les Fleurs du mal* the year after Heine died.

COMPASSION REQUIRES a strenuous effort and is hard
to sustain in the long run, and although the dingy apartment
in the rue d'Amsterdam remained an obligatory stop on the
itinerary of visiting German intellectuals, Heine's local
friends and acquaintances, much as they deplored his condition, showed up less and less often as his agony stretched
from weeks into months and from months into years. There
were, of course, those who remained faithful. Caroline
Jaubert, for one, whose *Souvenirs* testify to a rare independent spirit combining genuine sympathy with an incor-
ruptible intelligence. While she never ceased to pay tribute
to Heine's amazing courage, she would not let herself be
charmed into ignoring some of his flaws, such as his cruel
mockery, directed at his friends as often as at his enemies—"What are friends for if not to forgive me?"—
and his tendency to get carried away by his own sense of
humor, belaboring a point until wit turned to water. "This
mind, compared for its incisive and unfettered quality so
often—and for good reason—to that of Voltaire, did not
in conversation always have the light touch that is truly
French; he was unable to let go of a subject and instead
doggedly clung to it with his teeth." Gérard de Nerval
remained devoted, but even while his varied writings—
essays, novels, poetry, travelogues—were at last being collected in the early 1850s and published in book form to
considerable acclaim, his lucid interludes became increasingly rare; during one of his visits, his behavior turned so
bizarre that he had to be taken directly to the asylum, where
he remained for several weeks at Heine's expense. Théo-

phile Gautier was another of Heine's steady visitors. Poet, novelist, author of the notorious *Mademoiselle de Maupin* and all-around *homme de lettres* who for some forty years produced a weekly column of literary criticism, he had been one of Heine's staunchest admirers from the very beginning and remained a faithful friend to the end, though it is not entirely clear if Heine ever fully appreciated either the author or the man.

There were others. Dumas *père* came to see him, so did Berlioz. But after the brief triumph and excitement of the *Romanzero* Heine felt more isolated than ever before; the walls of the sickroom began to close in on him, and time seemed to grind to a halt.

> *Wie langsam kriechet sie dahin,*
> *Die Zeit, die schauderhafte Schnecke!*
> *Ich aber, ganz bewegungslos*
> *Blieb ich hier auf demselben Flecke.*
>
> *In meine dunkel Zelle dringt*
> *Kein Sonnenstrahl, kein Hoffnungsschimmer,*
> *Ich weiss, nur mit der Kirchhofsgruft*
> *Vertausch ich dies fatale Zimmer.*

*(How slowly it creeps along, Time, that repulsive monster of a snail, yet I remain motionless altogether, pinned to the selfsame spot. No sunbeam, no glimmer of hope enter my dark cell, and I know that it is only with the grave that I'll exchange this fatal room.)*

If the frenetic experience with the *Romanzero* had left him exhausted, it had also taught him that keeping his mind occupied and engaging his energy to the utmost offered the only hope of survival in any meaningful sense of the word.

The apartment, originally chosen because it was cheap, had turned into an antechamber of his private hell; he had come to hate it not so much for its perennial darkness and lack of space but rather because of the constant noise from the neighbors who, he came to feel, were deliberately hammering on top and next door to him around the clock and wrecking what was left of his delicate nervous system. He beseeched Mathilde to look for another place, preferably farther from the center of town, but somehow the beloved child-wife never made any serious attempt to do so. The ferocious heatwave during the summer of 1852, while adding greatly to Heine's distress, also served Mathilde as an excuse for not engaging in any activity more strenuous than shopping. She had grown very heavy, and aside from having trouble getting around, she was not at all eager to move to some outlying arrondissement remote from the as yet pre-Haussmannian but already grand boulevards where she presumably spent her days shopping for lace, an abiding and expensive passion.

What Mathilde really did during those long afternoons is something that will never be known and has long ceased to matter, if it ever did in the first place. Shopping for lace may indeed have been all that ever filled her life and time, but if Heine occasionally let himself think otherwise, he wisely kept it to himself. She was a flighty young woman in her thirties forced to share her life with a cripple, she seemed to be doing it cheerfully enough, and the least he could do was to try and make it up to her by indulging her foolish extravagances; paying her bills was the one way he had left of asserting his manhood.

He also put up with her choice of companions. The insipid and ailing Pauline Rogue had gradually become part of the household, one more mouth to feed, but a far more obnoxious creature was Mathilde's bosom pal Elise Arnault, a woman of decidedly dubious antecedents whose husband, an illiterate go-getter of the crudest stripe, had made money running a small circus. His booming smugness made Heine want to strangle him whenever the couple dropped in for a visit, which was all too often. Their only redeeming asset was their little daughter Alice, of whom Heine was very fond and to whom he liked to read fairy tales.

Did he ever fear being abandoned by Mathilde? We don't know, and chances are he did not, either. But on the evidence of some of his last poems he seems to have retained a deep and genuine tenderness for her till the very end, and worries over her future continued to rank high among his incentives for work and his motives for staying alive. With the *Romanzero* out of the way and scant prospects for another major work in the foreseeable future, he began to cast about for some other means of keeping his name in the public eye and hit upon the idea of collecting the articles he had written for the *Augsburger Allgemeine Zeitung* between 1831 and 1844 and publishing them—suitably updated with the benefit of hindsight—as a historical perspective on France in the age of Louis Philippe.

It would have been a rather formidable project even for an author in the best of health; for Heine, given his condition, it constituted a brazen challenge to fate.

For all his skepticism, Heine clung to the hoary superstition about blood being thicker than water, his sentimental attachment to the idea of the family made the blows that came to him from within its heaving bosom all the more painful. With his sister, Charlotte, one year younger and thoroughly unremarkable except for living to the age of ninety-nine, he maintained affectionate relations throughout his life despite her marriage to a dull, self-righteous Hamburg merchant of pronounced reactionary tendencies. His two brothers, five and seven years younger respectively, were no part of his childhood and later entered his life only as sentimental clichés with whom he had nothing in common other than a set of parents. Gustav, the older, trained as an agronomist, joined the Austrian Army after going bankrupt, and eventually became the editor of a staunchly progovernment newspaper in Vienna; in due course, his editorial stance and personal pomposity earned him a baronetcy. Maximilian, the younger, served as a physician in the Russian Army and settled in St. Petersburg, where he rose to a high position at the imperial court, wrote medical treatises, and married a socially prominent widow. Heine had not seen either of them for decades; and while distance may not necessarily make the heart grow fonder, it can easily foster unrealistic expectations. Thus he looked forward with great excitement to visits from what to all intents and purposes were two strangers whom in the course of the years he had come to idealize after a fashion, Gustav as a hard-nosed businessman with a heart of gold, Max as the gentle and omniscient healer. Needless to say, neither was able to live up to his image.

Gustav was first to make the pilgrimage. A fussy, impetuous, and self important bureaucrat, he brought along his wife, a snobbish and hypochondriacal shrew to whom Heine took an instant dislike cordially reciprocated by his sister-in-law. In his published account of the meeting, Gustav notes that in spite of preliminary warnings he was at first dumbstruck at his brother's appearance and simply unable to speak for quite some time. The face alone seemed unchanged, though ennobled, the image of a suffering Christ. ("Why not?" Heine is reported to have said. "He, too, was just another Jew.") "After exchanging some memories of childhood," Gustav reported, "I asked him if it was true what they said about his having become a believer.

'I'm all piety,' he said, 'and I pray to God every day for Him to change your political outlook.' I thereupon jokingly remarked that I was happy to have heard him mention God in this context, which led me to conclude that he was no longer an atheist. At the same time, I seriously urged him to further the cause of the faith by publicly acknowledging his change of mind. Whereupon he replied: 'The great white elephant of the King of Siam could not care less whether or not a little mouse in the rue d'Amsterdam in Paris believes in his grandeur and wisdom.' "

In practical terms, the visit qualified as something of a success. Torn between pride in his brother's fame and disapproval of his politics, Gustav honestly endeavored to be helpful. He intervened quite successfully on his behalf in the matter of the Prague gasworks and advanced him money on several occasions, but when Heine rather unwisely asked him to pursue face-to-face negotiations with Campe, his threats and overbearing manners so outraged the publisher that he came close to breaking off relations once again. Nevertheless, as a result of this meeting, the first in twenty-one years, the brothers had at least on the surface established something resembling a fraternal relationship, prodding Gustav's conscience sufficiently for him to assume certain responsibilities. And while he may not always have been his brother's most effective representative, he was probably the most honest one.

On the other hand, it quickly became clear to Heine that, grateful though he may have felt for Gustav's support, the two of them had absolutely nothing in common. But he consoled himself with the thought that while Gustav was essentially a government functionary with a ninny for a wife and a file cabinet for a mind, Max in St. Petersburg was a man of the world, a doctor, a writer, and a bachelor to boot (he later married the widow of the Czar's personal physician and added a *von* to his name.)

Max, alias Chickenshit—the nickname lovingly conferred upon him in childhood by his oldest brother—arrived in mid-July, the hottest time of the year, for a three-week stay. A pompous gentleman of quiet disposition, he inspected French sanitary installations, pronounced himself favorably impressed—this was in 1852!—on the numerous *crèches* established by the government for the children of working mothers, and in all other respects conducted himself like a benevolent visiting dignitary, a very far cry from the soulmate and intellectual equal Heine had hoped for. Still, both behaved in a more or less civilized fashion, and it was not until October, almost three months after Max's departure, that Heine gave vent to his profound disappointment about the visit:

I am sorry that everything has to end in such a bad way, but I remain calm and resigned. The presence of my brother Max here in Paris did not do much for me. He told me endless stories about what a great man he was, but he wouldn't listen to me for even two minutes, and he left before I was ever able to say anything to him. He most certainly did not impress me. I am not fooled by empty phrases, and basically all I saw was a tired soul that had invented all sorts of phony feelings for itself and that yet stank of egotism. He told me how happy he made his housekeeper, how happy he made his servants and his coachman, how happy he made the coachman's wife and how he even provided for her future, how he offers free consultations, and how all of St. Petersburg honors and appreciates him. In short, he is a benefactor of mankind, and people like that make me sick. I much prefer real bad guys, who at least are *something*. I so admired that boy, and now I am not even allowed to take that illusion with me into my grave. He is and remains nothing other than Max Chickenshit.

The fact that he wrote these lines to his brother Gustav testifies both to the depth of his rage and to that impetuous lack of discretion which even his sporadic efforts at saintly detachment were never quite able to overcome.

•

In the meantime, he had made preliminary efforts both to get copies of his articles from the editor of the *Augsburger Allgemeine Zeitung* and to sell the project to Campe. Neither proved an easy task. There were many gaps in the newspaper's files, whole series survived only in single copies and had to be laboriously copied out by hand, and almost all the articles had in various degrees been cut and slashed by the censors. Heine himself had preserved few of the original drafts, and it soon became clear that restoring and updating the material as a whole would involve a monumental effort, especially on the part of someone half blind and unable even to sit up.

Somehow the effort as such failed to intimidate him, in part at least because Heine vastly underestimated the time and energy required. On the contrary, he saw it as yet another chance to keep his mind gainfully occupied while at the same time furthering his literary career. "I've been given to understand," he wrote to Campe in June, "that the public is now much more interested in social and political conditions than in hoary literary gossip. I tend to agree and have in mind a book that would represent the fruit and harvest of my quarter-century of exploring Paris . . . After the *Romanzero*, so my friends tell me, the public expects a work of prose from me." But the canny publisher smelled a very dead rat and said so in no uncertain terms, especially after Heine hit him for a 6,000-mark advance, the same amount as he had received for the *Romanzero*. Campe pointed out that nothing fades as fast as yesterday's news and that he could not conceive of an audience for a collection of twenty-year-old newspaper clippings. Heine, deeply hurt in his pride—or at least pretending to be—

countered that a writer such as himself would never, ever step before his public with a mere rehash of faded old clippings; what he had in mind was to use the articles only as the basis for a long-range historical and cultural perspective on the reign of Louis Philippe.

Campe didn't bite. As usual, he complained of having lost money on the *Romanzero* and offered to print the book at Heine's own expense in a sort of vanity-press arrangement, serving merely as the distributor—an offer which, given Heine's standing and their long association, was tantamount to a slap in the face. Negotiations dragged on for much of the rest of the year, and the personal intervention —or interference —on the part of the other two Heine brothers did nothing to ease the tension. In the end, a compromise of sorts was struck. Campe agreed to pay 6,000 marks, but for three volumes rather than one. A battle-weary Heine reluctantly accepted the offer.

IT WOULD BE fatuous to maintain that throughout the eight years of his terminal illness Heine battled death with unwavering determination; there was many a time when he seemed ready to give up a struggle of whose ultimate hopelessness he needed no convincing. But few poets of his or any other age lived with death for so long in such close quarters and on such intimate terms, and it was this undramatic, understated familiarity that marked the work of his final phase and that also, one suspects, accounts for much of the rejection it encountered in its time. The nineteenth century was quite as uncomfortable as our own in dealing with the stark vision of Death without first swaddling him—or her; as Heine pointed out, *der Tod* in German is *la Mort* in French—in euphemism and sentiment; the nightly gore on our living-room screens is merely another way, infinitely more sophisticated, of hiding Death's true face. Heine, for his part, in what he called the "poems of his agony," refused to oblige. After the flurry about the *Romanzero* had abated, he—more by instinct than out of any conscious decision—settled into a routine that his highly variable health, his surroundings, and the natural sequence of darkness and light in the pre-electric age imposed upon him and that he more or less observed until the final moments of his life. The nights were uniformly bad; he habitually got very little sleep, and four in the morning is a time when pain, terror, and desperation reach a crescendo that easily defies both opium and self-irony. Heine, however, found one remedy that worked for him; this was the hour when he wrote, or rather composed, his poetry, a form of prayer whose healing magic reveals the one and only true nature of his faith. He was many things to many people, including himself; but above all else, he was a poet, first, last, and always.

With daybreak the other self emerged. There was the usual commotion in the household, the morning toilette, the struggle to down what passed for a nutritious breakfast, and then the wait for the secretary, whose arrival signaled the start of the literally prosaic activities of the day once the poetic harvest of the night had been duly transcribed. The position was a crucial one to Heine, the equivalent of his eyes and ears, but for years it was filled by a succession of mostly nondescript hacks, the exceptions being Karl Hillebrand, later a well-known essayist, and Richard Reinhardt, who introduced himself in 1849 as a friend of Marx and Engels and gradually assumed the management of many of Heine's business affairs as well. Efficient as well as officious, nearly bilingual, he made himself quite indispensable for a number of years and proved especially helpful with the nightmarish muddle of the old newspaper articles into which Heine was endeavoring to breathe new life. It eventually became clear that nothing short of a complete rewrite would give them the sort of structural unity that Heine felt was imperative for what he knew would be the final publication of his lifetime. The task proved complicated far beyond anything he had envisaged, and the frequent reminders of imminent mortality added an urgency to it that often threw him into a frenzy yet at the same time served to mobilize whatever reserves he had left. They turned out to be formidable beyond all expectations.

The prisoner of the rue d'Amsterdam paid less and less attention to contemporary French politics beyond the walls of his cell. They elicited an occasional wisecrack or a contemptuous snort, but no emotional commitment or intellectual engagement. He had minimized the uprisings of 1848, in part out of an understandable preoccupation with the onset of his paralysis and in part because the true significance of the events only began to emerge in retrospect. The election of the rather enigmatic Louis-Napoléon in December 1848 pleased him simply because the new President happened to be the son of Napoleon Bonaparte's mildly insane brother Louis, the King of Holland, and emotionally Heine was still enough of a Bonapartist to hope that perhaps some of the uncle's magic might have survived in the nephew.

Under the new constitution, the chief executive, elected to a four-year term, could not succeed himself. Louis-Napoléon solved that problem by a coup d'état on December 2, 1851—the anniversary of his uncle's victory at Austerlitz. He arrested all members of the opposition, rewrote the constitution, and organized a plebiscite which, on December 21, ratified his proposal for a ten-year presidential term by a popular vote of 7 million for and 600,000 against. Another plebiscite months later, on November 21, 1852, completed the gestation of the counter-revolution by reestablishing the absolutist monarchy, with the Prince-President henceforth known as the Emperor Napoléon III. Like many others, Heine by this time had changed his mind about the new Emperor, whose inner cabinet consisted of a clique of rapacious crooks and who immediately imposed an absolutist regime based on the combined—and formidable—power of the army and the police. And yet the abrupt collapse of the opposition may have had less to do with active repression than with a surge of prosperity set off by the Industrial Revolution. That the rising tide lifts all boats is manifestly true when taken literally; as an economic metaphor it amounts to little more than a mindless slogan—a lot of those boats capsize and get swamped, while others turn airborne and head for the stars. Nonetheless, the living standards of the bourgeoisie rose significantly under the Second Empire, and the imperial government reaped the credit for it, all the more so since in stark contrast to its predecessors it at least made a pretense of paying attention to the problems of the working class as well. But what ultimately shaped the evolution of full-fledged capitalism were massive investments in transportation and real estate and the increasing concentration of capital in major banking houses such as the Rothschilds, the Pereires, and the Foulds (the last Heine's enemies-by-marriage). The great department stores—Bon Marché, Printemps, Samaritaine—first opened their doors, and the railroad network rapidly expanded sixfold, from 3,000 to 18,000 kilometers. But in the eyes of posterity the most radical change was the spectacular transformation of Paris itself from a still semi-medieval albeit vastly picturesque capital to the modern metropolis we know today.

It was to an amazing degree the work of one man, although the Emperor himself provided the initiative, laid down the broader political aims of the reconstruction, and deserves credit for appointing a multifaceted genius who could not only do the job but also came up with ways of financing it without raising taxes; the modern bond issue as much as the grand boulevards and the Paris sewers go back in large measure to Georges-Eugène Haussmann.

Born in 1809, he earned a law degree and served as prefect in a number of provincial capitals before being appointed prefect of the Department of the Seine on June 22, 1853. Two weeks later he began an urban-renewal project that was not to see its like anywhere until after the air raids of the Second World War.

The goals as laid down by the Emperor combined politics,

aesthetics, and business: to begin with, a network of broad avenues and streets that could not easily be blocked by barricades and in which the troops could march abreast, with a clear field of fire ahead. Beyond that, there was the need to free the great monuments of the past—the Hôtel de Ville, the Louvre, Notre-Dame—from the clutter of ramshackle warrens that encroached upon them, and to provide easy access to the new railroad stations that brought thousands of travelers and tourists into the city. Haussmann proceeded with a ruthlessness that became legendary. He laid waste whole sections of Paris, triggering a frenzy of real-estate speculation. He acquired the Bois de Boulogne for the city and transformed it from a wild forest into the Emperor's idea of an English garden. And in 1854 he began the construction of the Paris sewers, a veritable underground city, as well as the 131-kilometer-long Dhuis aqueduct, which, for the first time, provided a sanitary substitute for the contaminated Seine water responsible for recurrent outbreaks of epidemics. Altogether the team of Emperor and Haussmann, which ruled supreme if not unreviled until 1870, was responsible for an astonishing amount of construction, from the Palais de Justice and the Hôtel Dieu to the Grand Opéra, the Halles, and the Temple, not to mention a large number of churches as well as the major bridges spanning the Seine.

That large-scale construction was preceded by destruction on an even larger scale goes without saying and accounts for most of the enmity Haussmann engendered. Romantics, historians, and the merely old deplored the disappearance of many a landmark and of the picturesque, semi-rural corners of the capital. The statesman Jules Ferry spoke for many of his generation when he wrote in 1868: "As for the old Paris, the Paris of Voltaire, of Diderot and Desmoulins, the Paris of 1830 and 1848, we weep for it with all the tears that come to our eyes as we see . . . the triumphant vulgarity, the terrible materialism that we bequeath to our children." The demolition of vast areas of urban slums left thousands of people homeless, most of whom were unable to afford the exorbitant rents charged by the owners of the new apartment buildings. But as Anatole France pointed out, both rich and poor alike had the right to sleep under the bridges.

Gradually Haussmann's enemies gathered strength, and in 1870, a year before his own downfall, the Emperor reluctantly dismissed him. But the fact remains that the miracle of modern Paris would have been unthinkable without him.

Most of these changes, political as well as architectural, left Heine reasonably indifferent; they took place in a world with which he had increasingly tenuous contact. But on April 1, 1853, the *Revue des Deux Mondes* published his essay *The Gods in Exile*. It is not at all clear when it was originally written; the basic idea—the victory of Christianity over the pagan gods and their shabby lives in a secular exile which has nothing in common with the demonic transformations ascribed to them by Christian superstition—is obviously a very old one which Heine had ridden even way back in his romantic period. But the exposition here, in which he deals with the fate of each individual god, is clever and often funny, and the climactic scene of a ragged, half-demented Jupiter marooned on a North Sea island and trading in rabbit skins is brilliantly rendered. The bulk of it may have actually been written in the spring. At any rate, the response of the French public was extremely gratifying, but a clumsy, flatfooted retranslation into German appeared a week later in the *Hamburger Nachrichten* and thoroughly spoiled his mood. It turned out to be merely the beginning of his problems. He had actually attempted to find a German publisher, but the rising reaction in post-'48 Germany made him more of a pariah than ever, and few newspapers were prepared to deal with him. Post-publication censorship was, if anything, even stricter under the rapidly expanding state bureaucracies with their reinforced police powers; but Campe still maintained semi-clandestine channels of distribution that not only got his books on the market but even fetched a premium. The tainted translation came out in book form on April 25 in Berlin, and in June no less than four pirated French editions appeared in Brussels. The corrupt German translation even appeared in a Philadelphia magazine called *Die Locomotive* published by one of Heine's future biographers, followed about two years later by a pirated edition of Heine's Collected Works published by a Philadelphia bookseller named John Weik. Pirated editions now began to appear all over the map, testimony to his growing international renown, but he fumed about the loss of income and demanded that Campe do something about it. Copyright laws being what they were, Heine had little recourse beyond some angry public protests in the papers.

Campe for his part had gone back to sulking, this time over Heine's demands for the advance on the collection of articles, in which he did not believe. His resilience, his resourcefulness, and on occasion even his courage are indisputable, but despite Campe's reputed charm he must have been a man singularly devoid of humanity to treat one of his most faithful and lucrative authors, of whose desperate condition he in the meantime had personally convinced himself, with the cold contempt he displayed time and again. In the latest round he informed Heine that friendship and business simply did not mix, a piece of advice which Heine for once was quick to follow, after a fashion. "I've taken good note of your latest slogan to the effect that friendship and business don't mix," he wrote to Campe in October 1853. "But how come, dear Campe, that every time you want a favor from me in the interest of your business you appeal to my friendship? Whereas I for my part, who could well do with some friendship in my position, invariably meet up only with the stern businessman whenever I ask for money. But so be it. I confess that all my life I indulged in a poetic delusion, but we shall now dispense with it. From now on, if we talk business, friendship won't be something you'll have to complain about . . . You'll be able to enjoy my friendship in all its purity, and the businessman will not be asked to bring any sacrifices."

MUCH OF THE REST of the year went into preparing the collection of old newspaper articles that was eventually published under the title *Lutezia*, the ancient Roman name for Paris. Whether or not it warranted what must have been a harrowing expenditure of energy and time is something no outsider is qualified to judge; Heine obviously believed wholeheartedly in the project and worked at it with a remarkably sustained enthusiasm, which was certainly at least part of its purpose.

*Lutezia* is Heine's longest prose work and has always presented problems even to his most indulgent and faithful readers and exegetes. Large parts of it read precisely like what they are—the faded clippings of old newspaper articles, albeit by one of the most brilliant stylists of the period. Many of them have the vitality and verve that characterize so much of Heine's writing, but most readers will probably feel that he fooled himself when he assured Campe that "the whole reads rather like a novel while at the same time it is a historical document" and that it contains "an intellectual treasure for those who would resuscitate political life in Germany." Heine was a poet with—for a poet—an extraordinarily broad range of interests in such prosaic fields as politics, human rights, philosophy, and economics, plus a smattering of prejudices in the arts, but one would be hard put to regard him very highly as either a historian or a journalist. What he mostly expressed were his opinions, usually trenchant and well-informed but defiantly subjective, frequently straying way off the topic and in any event subject to sudden change. In the revised version of the articles, moreover, he often yielded to the temptation of updating his views and thus endowing himself retrospectively with more foresight than he had actually demonstrated at the time, but such cosmetic readjustments for the sake of vanity seem easy enough to forgive.

Much more problematic is the focus on what at the time were the outstanding politicians—Thiers, Guizot, and above all King Louis Philippe himself. He had perceptive if often contradictory things to say about them all, but they had disappeared from the scene. As usual, however, he did not confine himself to politicians when it came to his version of character analysis, and among the minor gems of the collection is a report on the premiere of George Sand's *Cosima*, dated April 30, 1840, that deftly conveys the intricate relationship between the feminist author and the social forces arrayed against her.

Last night, after an almost two-month delay. . . . George Sand's *Cosima* finally opened at the Théâtre Français. Impossible to imagine to what lengths the notables and celebrities of this city . . . went in their efforts to attend this performance. The author's fame is so great that everyone was desperately eager to see the piece, but interests and passions other than mere curiosity were involved. The cabals, malice, and intrigues about to be mounted against the play were known well in advance . . . The daring author, whose novels offend the aristocracy as well as the bourgeoisie in about equal measure because of her "immoral and irreligious principles," was about to be punished on the occasion of her debut as a dramatist because, as I recently pointed out, the French aristocracy regards religion as a bulwark against the looming horrors of republicanism . . . while to the bourgeois the anti-matrimonial doctrines of a George Sand constitute an equally dangerous threat to their heads; they are afraid of being made to wear the sort of horns that married citizens would rather do without . . . Well, how then was it received, this drama by George Sand, the greatest author of the new France, this strangely lone genius honored even in Germany? Frankly, I am at a loss as to how to answer the question; the author's reputation may have thwarted some sinister plots that failed to materialize . . . But as to the actual staging, I can only report the worst. Except for the famous Dorval, who yesterday was neither better or worse than always, all the actors displayed their usual monotonous mediocrity . . . George Sand seems to have sensed how little her drama could expect from the exertions of the actors, and in a conversation with a German friend she remarked: "You see, the French are all of them born actors, and they play their roles with varying degrees of brilliance. But it is those with the least talent for acting who are the very ones to devote themselves to the theater." I myself have already remarked on the fact that public life in France, the parliamentary system and the political struggle, tend to absorb the best histrionic talent of the French and leave only the dregs of mediocrity for the actual stage. This, however, applies only to the men: the French stage is richly endowed with actresses of the highest caliber . . . the more easily able to develop their talents because male usurpation and repressive legislation excludes women in this country from all political positions and honors. And since they cannot exercise their talents in parliament, they make their entry into public life either via the Temples of Art or the Temples of Eros . . . or both at once, since the two trades are not as strictly separated as they are in Germany.

In 1854 he greatly amplified this notice by adding a detailed biography of George Sand, alias Aurora Dudevant née Dupin, and pays her a rather exorbitant dual compliment: not only is she the greatest woman writer, but her beauty compares favorably to that of the Venus de Milo. He even finds it in his heart to praise her two most famous lovers, the poet Alfred de Musset and "our much beloved

Frédéric Chopin." George Sand in prose and de Musset in verse "rank far above the so highly praised Victor Hugo, who, with his grimly stubborn, almost moronic persistence, has fooled the French and finally even himself into being taken for France's greatest poet. Is this really his own *idée fixe*? It certainly isn't ours. Oddly enough, his greatest deficiency is the lack of the very quality that is so common to the French and which they appreciate above all else: taste. He is wholly artificial, a liar . . . ice cold through and through like the devil to the touch according to the testimony of the witches . . . His enthusiasm is only a phantasmagoria, a calculated effusion without love, or rather, he loves no one but himself. He is an egotist, or to put it even more pointedly, a Hugotist."

In the end, *Lutezia* adds up to an extensive display of some of the best as well as the worst characteristics of Heine as a *feuilletoniste*. One does not have to agree with Karl Kraus's priggish and essentially anti-Semitic attack on him as the originator of the much-despised feuilleton—was there ever anything Karl Kraus did not despise, himself included?—to concede that Heine could be wildly digressive and discursive in his newspaper prose and that his wit often labored the point in the tortuously flatfooted manner hinted at by Caroline Jaubert. Yet at the same time the book also showcases some of his most brilliant aspects. He was in his way a social critic way ahead of his time, such as in the questions he raises about the "Pennsylvania system," i.e., the individual prison cells that were being introduced in France. In traveling in the provinces he discovered a country of whose existence, at least as a force in politics, few foreigners and not all that many French had been aware of at the time. He explored the struggle between church and state over education in terms that suggest why today, some 160 years later, the problem still resists a solution.

And, notably in the preface to the French edition, he defines his politics at the end of his life in what is probably the most coherent formulation he ever attempted: he believes that the future belongs to the Communists, the equivalent of the Nazarenes in Rome, a prospect which nonetheless fills him with apprehension and anguish when he thinks of a time when their calloused hands will destroy all the art and beauty of his world, and

some grocer will use even the pages of my *Book of Songs* to wrap coffee or snuff for the old women of the future. Alas, I foresee all of this, and I am seized by an unspeakable sadness when I think of the threat by the victorious proletariat to my verses, which will perish together with the entire old romantic world. And yet I must frankly admit that this same Communism, so inimical to all my interests and inclinations, casts a spell against which I am unable to defend myself. Two voices make themselves heard in its favor . . . The first is that of logic; "The Devil is a logician," said Dante. A terrible syllogism holds me in its ban, and if I cannot refute the premise that *all men have the right to eat*, then I must accept all of what follows from it . . . The second voice is even more powerful and infernal than the first: it is the voice of hate, of the hate I bear against a party of which Communism is the most terrible antagonist and which, for that reason, is our common enemy: I am speaking of the so-called representatives of German nationalism, of those false patriots whose love for the fatherland consists of nothing but an insane hatred of foreigners and neighbors, notably France. Yes, this trash, these heirs to the Teutomaniacs of 1815 who have merely updated their costume and had their ears clipped a little—I have despised and fought them all my life, and now that the sword is slipping from my dying hand, I feel comforted by the conviction that Communism, which will find them trying to block the way, will give them the coup de grâce . . . Hatred of the nationalist thugs could almost make me love the

Communists. They at least are not the kind of hypocrites who constantly spout religion and Christianity. True, they have no religion at all (no one is perfect) . . . but as their principal dogma they profess the most absolute cosmopolitanism, universal love for all people, and an egalitarian co-fraternity of all free citizens of this earth. This fundamental dogma is the same once preached by the Gospels, so that in truth and spirit the Communists are in fact more Christian than our Teutonic patriots.

Heine formed and delivered his opinions more on the basis of intuition than analysis, and on the whole the free-wheeling, creative intuition of the poet proved far more accurate in its long-range vision than stacks of learned tomes. The uncompromising hatred of German ultra-nationalism forged in his youth and reinforced along every stage of his life transcended any mere ideological stance and became one of the most consistent attributes of his personality, a gut feeling that enabled him to sense the nature of the beast long before it ever fully surfaced. And if he vastly misjudged its strength in relation to Communism, he was far from alone.

•

One of the controversies surrounding *Lutezia* concerned the role of his secretary Richard Reinhardt. Competent and efficient, unlike most of the scribblers engaged by Heine more or less ad hoc at one time or another, he started working for Heine around 1850, at first on a once-a-week basis and gradually more and more often as Heine's forces declined. In person he was, from all accounts, a rather surly and pigheaded individual, anything but a charmer, but he did get things done, and soon not only took dictation but also handled a good deal of the business correspondence more or less on his own. In fact, it was Reinhardt who conducted at least part of the negotiations with Campe on Heine's behalf.

In retrospect one cannot help but suspect that from the very start he may also have had an agenda of his own. For one thing, as a friend of Marx and Engels and a member of their Workers Party—which, given the size of the party at the time, qualified him as a member of their inner circle—he kept up the contact between them and Heine, though it seems more than doubtful that he—any more than anyone else—would have been in a position to influence Heine's attitude toward Communism. For another, he had literary ambitions, considered himself a poet, and at the very least must have expected to benefit in some way from Heine's imminent demise. He was indisputably of great service, and it is to be assumed that Heine appreciated his efficiency, but one gets the impression that at the personal level their relationship remained distant if not downright chilly, and the manner and cause of the final breach between them testifies to a rather startling lack of mutual sympathy in spite of an ongoing relationship of nearly five years' duration.

Reinhardt also happened to be virtually bilingual, and it was largely he who translated *Lutezia* into French. He received no credit for it; the French version appeared without listing the name of a translator, making it appear as though Heine had done the job himself. Reinhardt, by way of compensation, demanded that he be appointed Heine's literary executor and, when met with Heine's instant and categorical refusal, accused him of rank ingratitude. Whereupon Heine summarily fired him. In a letter to Campe the following day he coolly reported that "yesterday I was forced to take full measure of the temperamental differences that exist between me and my former secretary, and the adjective 'former' will itself tell you that we had to separate."

The irony of it all being that the stubborn and pedantic German, had he in fact been put in charge of Heine's literary estate, would probably have done a far better job than those to whom it was eventually entrusted or who robbed, stole, bought, sold, scattered, and destroyed it. He certainly could not have done any worse.

FOR ONE THING, we might have known a good deal more about Heine's mysterious *Memoirs*—if in fact they existed.

He talked and wrote *about* them ever since he was in his early twenties, still feeding at Uncle Salomon's stable, the bumbling shlemiel of a nephew incapable of adding two and two but whom one had to support because he was *family*. Like father, like son. The trouble with him was that on top of being no good at business or anything else that mattered, he had a highly inflated opinion of himself and constantly needed to be reminded of his pervasive insignificance. Most particularly once he took an interest in Amalie. She was Salomon's older daughter, and Harry the Lip was definitely not what the King had in mind as a son-in-law.

The unrequited love of the budding poet for his plain but rich cousin—and, a couple of years later, for her better-looking and equally rich younger sister Theresa—has been mythologized into one of the great heartbreaks of literary history and the tragic inspiration for many of the poems in the *Book of Songs*. Heine himself, discreet to a fault when it came to his innermost feelings, only obliquely fed this myth of a lifelong passion. As early as October 1827, on the occasion of a meeting with the by then safely married Amalie, he wrote to his friend Varnhagen: "This morning I am about to visit a fat lady whom I have not seen in eleven years and with whom I am once supposed to have been in love. Her name is Mrs. Friedländer from Königsberg, so to speak a cousin of mine. The husband of her choice I already saw yesterday, by way of an apéritif . . . The world is stupid and insipid and unpleasant and smells of dried violets."

A pose, perhaps, but all the signs point to a much different interpretation of this putative heartbreak as simply part of a concentrated assault on a gifted young man's self-esteem. What truly hurt was not Amalie's rejection of his suit so much as the Family's contemptuous sneer at the mere thought of it. That Heine was exquisitely sensitive to any slight, real or imagined, is certainly true; but in the light of their subsequent behavior, deliberate cruelty on the part of Salomon Heine and members of his household would seem highly probable, the more so since Cousin Harry, though he may not have known how to take it, certainly knew how to dish it out. It hardly matters, however; paranoids do have enemies, and although Heine undoubtedly dramatized these youthful sufferings throughout his life, they must have contained a core of genuine long-acting poison. In 1850 he could still write to his brother Gustav with what sounds like absolute conviction: "Since you now have a vague notion of the type of people on whose generosity I had to depend, you will understand that in addition to my physical suffering I had to put up with a moral torment about which I don't want to talk today, since the mere thought of it upsets me; I may tell you about this wound some other time, or perhaps I won't either, because it all ties into the origins of my illness, which was caused by a shock such as few human beings ever experienced on this earth."

There is nothing more natural than the young man, bent on getting even with his philistine tormentors, deciding to attack —or threatening to—with the one weapon he already wields with consummate mastery—his pen. Heine was twenty-five when he first wrote to a friend: "When someday you read my memoirs with their description of a gang of people from Hamburg, a few of whom I love, several whom I hate, and the majority whom I despise, you will better understand me."

Throughout the years that followed there were scattered references to the *Memoirs*, but they assumed concrete substance only in 1837, when he proposed to introduce a collected edition of his works with an autobiographical study, "a book, a great and important one encompassing all of European life as well as all the real and symbolic figures that belong to it, the result of all my peripatetic studies in all countries and situations." To Campe he wrote a few weeks later: "Day and night I am busy with my great book, the novel of my life . . . You know I am not in the habit of bragging, and I can already guarantee you something extraordinary, because I know my public and know exactly which people and events it wants to be instructed and entertained about." He asked for a sizable advance, which Campe refused, and in the months that followed the *Memoirs* turned into a sort of blunderbuss loaded with manure that he kept pointing at various figures he considered hostile. In September, begging Uncle Salomon to resume friendly relations and forgive him for sins he was not even aware of having committed, he could not help ending a cloyingly humbling epistle on a note of characteristic fustian hardly designed to inspire conciliatory moves: "What still keeps me upright is pride in my innate spiritual supremacy and the awareness that no one else in the world could wreak more powerful vengeance with fewer strokes of the pen than I, should I ever want to get even for all the open and secret misery being inflicted upon me." And so on through the years. In December 1837 he told Campe that he had dropped all work on the project, yet three years later, in September 1840, he assured him that "even if I were to die today, there are already four volumes of my autobiography or memoirs that will represent my views and intentions and be valued by posterity for their historical material, the faithful representation of the mysterious transitional crisis. The new generation will also want to see the shitty diapers that were its first covering."

The issue flared up again during the inheritance feud in 1845, when Carl Heine offered to pay half the promised pension provided he was given a chance to censor the *Memoirs*. Heine eventually committed himself orally not to write anything damaging about his late uncle and made it known that he had destroyed substantial parts of the manuscript of his own volition, but like a jack-in-the-box it popped up time and again—in four large boxes, to be precise, if we are to believe Meissner, who claimed to have seen a substantial manuscript on his last visit in 1854. Other visitors were more skeptical. The young German author Ludwig Kalisch on a visit to Heine in January 1850 mentioned that his public was still waiting impatiently for the *Memoirs*. "I have every intention of publishing them," Heine said, "but I don't know if I'll manage to finish them. I dictate almost every day, which is a terrible strain . . . I have burned many of my manuscripts, because they no longer conformed to my current convictions. Unfortunately," he added with a sigh, "I've burned too much. It happened in one of those dark moments where suicidal thoughts become irresistible. Too bad. There were good things among them. Peace be to their ashes." "I kept silent," Kalisch continued, "because I simply didn't believe in this auto-da-fé. Heine was not the sort of man who would keep manuscripts for years, only to burn them in the end because they no longer expressed his views. No poet ever felt more partial to the children of his Muse, and he would not deny a single one among them . . . Even a mere bad joke he didn't have the heart to abandon; those not fit to print he would repeat over and over till they became commonly known."

But a note to Campe in March 1854 about a new version

of the *Memoirs* sounds considerably more convincing: "Herr Trittau will have already told you that I have heroically tackled an entirely new version of my *Memoirs*, and I hope to see them published as the crown of my writings. It took heroism on my part to start from scratch rather than patch up the old material, and barring major distractions, I hope to have a large part finished by the end of the year. Since I now know what I am not allowed to say, I can write with great ease, and nothing will prevent me from launching the finished product even in my lifetime."

The image of a great poet knowing what he is "not allowed to say," of having knuckled under to blackmail from a few fatuous, priggish halfwits, makes for some rather melancholy thoughts. If the threatened loss of his pension was enough to make him practice self-censorship, how would this "lifelong fighter for freedom" have stood up a century later to pressures of an altogether different order? No way of telling. But it is my guess that he would have found it easy enough to resist Hitler. Hitler, after all, was not part of the Family.

•

As for whether or not the *Memoirs* ever actually existed, were destroyed, or may yet be moldering in some attic, scholarly opinion is divided to this day, though most experts incline toward the belief that members of the family got hold of the manuscript after Heine's death and destroyed it. The evidence is far from clear. Meissner, negotiating with Mathilde on behalf of Campe, claims to have seen a 600-page manuscript—not as large as it sounds, considering Heine's of necessity huge handwriting—which at that point she refused to sell on Campe's terms. Aided by a slimy shyster of a lawyer, she peddled Heine manuscripts for a number of years, at one point even persuading Count Metternich, of all people, to advocate the purchase by the Austrian government of the very manuscripts which, in his former role as head of that government, he had made a special point of banning throughout the realm. But the Ministry squelched the idea, and the Family finally made Mathilde an offer she apparently could not refuse. The text of the *Memoirs* published by Campe in 1884 as supplement to the Collected Works has obviously been badly mutilated, presumably by the gangsters to whom Heine had the misfortune of being related.

•

We will probably never know why a man who unhesitatingly defied the Prussian and Austrian censors, ridiculed radicals and reactionaries alike, and seldom backed away from a fight let himself be intimidated and in effect silenced by what, perhaps not without reason, he saw as a conspiracy by his extended family. The special, not to say peculiar, filial relationship to Uncle Salomon and the symbolic significance of Salomon's gesture in disinheriting him has already been alluded to. But by now Salomon was long since dead and buried; and although Heine, resorting to his private version of poetic license, would occasionally wax nostalgic about the alleged close friendship between him and his cousin in their younger days—of which there is no evidence whatsoever, though he did bravely nurse Carl when he came down with the cholera during a visit to Paris—Salomon's son was a decorticate bully with no perceptible capacity for human relations. The story of a premarital affair between Heine and Carl's wife seems highly doubtful and in any case scarcely relevant. And yet, with relentless brutality this troglodyte millionaire managed to bludgeon his cousin into accepting the sort of censorship Heine would never have tolerated from the King of Prussia. True, Heine needed money, and he did want to provide for Mathilde, but neither reason strikes me as sufficient to explain this total surrender of basic principles on the part of a poet and author who, whatever his other problems, never had a doubt about the lasting value of his work. The puzzle will probably remain unsolved; we are never going to be able to trace Heine's emotional entanglement with his family all the way back to its poisoned roots, any more than we are likely to discover just what it was that, again with poetic hyperbole, he referred to as "a shock such as few human beings ever experienced on this earth."

What he himself tells us about his childhood contains at best the barest outline of the facts, colored in by a very lively imagination. The closest we can come to the glacial origins of his universe are, I suspect, those dutifully affectionate bulletins full of irrelevant banter he dispatched at regular intervals to his mother, the person who at one point must have presided over it. "As regards the state of my health," reads a rather typical missive of December 3, 1853, "it continues as usual, and I truly do not know what I could possibly add to the eloquent report of one Canonicus Karthümmelchen of long ago: I still suffer from gas, and consequently from cramps caused by it, which do not, however, as in the case of my late father, affect the stomach. I hope you all live in peace and harmony. I am quite serene and let five be an even number. I did not achieve anything in this world, but it could have been even worse. This is how half-beaten dogs comfort themselves."

•

It was, Heine maintained, Mathilde and the Goddess of Poetry that kept him alive through the endless summer of 1853, the dreadful winter that followed and the spring of which he saw nothing but the changing patterns of light. Partly true, no doubt. But considering the vast amount of work he accomplished, the number of letters he sent out, and the steady stream of visitors, both welcome and unwelcome, he received during that period, it seems obvious that at least during daylight hours he did not leave himself much leeway for self-pity or other suicidal pursuits.

It was the night he reserved for confrontations with death.

•

Lucy Austin, who as a little girl on vacation in Boulogne with her mother, a fervent Germanophile and Heine devotee, had met the poet and been utterly captivated by the very special attention he always paid to children in general and little girls in particular, went to see him again years later, after her marriage to Lord Duff-Cordon, and left a moving description of their reunion:

I never saw him again till I went to Paris three years ago, when I heard that he was dying and very poor. I sent my name, and a message that if he chanced to remember the little girl to whom he told *Märchen* years ago at Boulogne, I should like to see him. He sent for me directly, remembered every little incident, and all the people who were in the same inn; a ballad I had sung, which recounted the tragical fate of Ladye Alice and her humble lover, Giles Collins, and ended by Ladye Alice taking only one spoonful of the gruel, "With sugar and spices so rich," while after her decease, "The parson licked up the rest." This diverted Heine extremely, and he asked after the *person* who drank the gruel directly.

I for my part could hardly speak to him, so shocked was I by his appearance. He lay on a pile of mattresses, his body wasted so that it seemed no bigger than a child under the sheet which covered him—the eyes closed, and the face altogether like the most painful and wasted *Ecce Homo* ever painted by some old German painter. His voice was weak and I was astonished at the animation with which he talked—evidently his mind had wholly survived his body. He raised his powerless eyelids with his thin white fingers, and exclaimed: *"Gott, die kleine Lucie ist gross geworden und hat einen Mann; das ist eigen."* [God, little Lucy has grown up and got herself a husband, how strange.] He then earnestly asked if I was happy and contented, and begged me to bring my husband to see him. He said again he hoped I was happy now, as I had always been such a merry child. I answered that I was no longer so merry as the *kleine Lucie* had been, but very happy and contented, and he said: "How nice. It makes one feel good to see a woman for a change who doesn't nurse a wounded heart. Unlike the women here, who in the end fail to realize that what is wrong with them is that they have no heart at all."

I saw him two or three times a week during a two-months stay in Paris, and found him always full of lively conversation and interest in everything, and of his old undisguised vanity, pleased to receive bad translations of his works, and anxious beyond measure to be well translated into English. He offered me the copyright of all his works as a gift, and said he would give me *carte-blanche* to cut out all I thought necessary on my own account or that of the English public . . .

On the whole, I never saw a man bear such horrible pain and misery in so perfectly unaffected a manner. He complained of his sufferings and was pleased to see tears in my eyes and then at once set to work to make me laugh heartily, which pleased him just as much. He neither paraded his anguish nor tried to conceal it or to put on any stoical airs; I also thought him far less sarcastic, more hearty, more indulgent, and altogether pleasanter than ever. After a few weeks he begged me not to tell him when I was going, for that he could not bear to say *Lebewohl auf ewig*, or to hear it, and repeated that I had come as *ein schöner gütiger Todesengel*, to bring him greetings from youth and from Germany, and to dispel all the *bösen französischen Gedanken*. When he spoke German to me he called me *Du* and used the familiar expressions and turns of language which Germans use to a child; in French I was *Madame* and *vous*. It was evident that I recalled some happy time of life to his memory, and that it was a great relief to him to

talk German and to consider me still as a child . . . The impression
he made on me was so deep that I had great difficulty to restrain
my tears till I had left the room the last few times I saw him, and
shall never forget the sad pale face and eager manner of poor
Heine.

READING HEINE's letters, his poems, and the accounts by various of his visitors in those final years of his life, one is struck by the one overwhelming impression they all convey without ever quite spelling it out—his immense loneliness. Even in his teens he very much kept his distance, and it was certainly no accident if, for one reason or another, he had long since broken with every one of the friends of his youth. This left him with countless acquaintances and a host of enemies but not a single human being with whom he could truly share his thoughts and feelings; certainly his wife did not qualify as a companion, but he could probably never have sustained any other kind of marital or pseudo-marital relationship. As long as he was still in reasonably good health, however, he quite successfully transformed his very isolation into a source of pride, part of his self-image as the truculent Hellenic demiurge upholding the virtues of truth and beauty. It seems highly improbable that a man whose razor-sharp intelligence and exquisite sense of irony animate almost every page he ever wrote could have failed to see the more absurd aspects of this defensive posture, and it certainly did not protect him from his painfully repressed need for love. But not until he was bedridden and paralyzed did the loneliness become yet another scourge, one most likely inflicted upon him by an irate Jehovah determined to remind him of his origins. Hellene, indeed.

Moreover, the lack of any close, reliable friends became a serious handicap in his increasingly complicated relations with the outside world and the sheer business of staying

alive. His brother Max, whom for years he had fantasized
about from a distance as a potential soulmate, had on close
contact turned out to be an amiable twit with no soul to
speak of. Ironically it was brother Gustav, in every respect
his very opposite and with whom he had absolutely nothing
in common other than a mother remote in every sense of
the word, who felt motivated to take on certain responsibilities in the management of Heine's affairs. He was tact-
less, pigheaded, aggressive, and almost wrecked Heine's
relations with Campe for good and ever, but he basically
meant well and proved helpful in many ways.

What neither he nor anyone else could provide was a
touch of human warmth, of genuine companionship and
mutual trust that would have not only made this dreary
existence a bit more bearable but also given the dying poet
someone to lean on for disinterested advice and unconditional support. In the circumstances, his obsessive concern
with money once again assumed dimensions far beyond the
mere practical ones.

This automatically put him into a very poor bargaining
position, something Campe was instantly ready to exploit
to the hilt. Shrewdly reading his author like an open book
and not reluctant to squeeze out what little blood was left
in that pitiable skeleton, the publisher categorically turned
down Heine's demand for a 6,000-mark advance for *Lutezia*
even though he knew that at least one competitor had offered to top that amount. He evidently felt sure he could
count on what he must have thought of as Heine's naïveté.
("When it comes to business," he is reported to have said,
"Heine is an idiot.") Naïveté there undoubtedly was, and
as a businessman Heine had quite conclusively demonstrated his incompetence already in his teens, but what
made him put up with Campe was something else altogether, an emotional bond—almost totally one-sided—in

which the monetary transactions became the principal measure of paternal affection.

There were, to be sure, practical considerations for not switching publishers at this late stage in his life. Aside from preferring the devil he knew, he was eager to have all his works appear in one unified Collected Edition, which would have been impossible for at least ten years if another publisher held the copyright to some of the final volumes. But in a spate of rather uncharacteristically abject letters Heine kept assuring Campe of his devotion, thereby undercutting what little room for bargaining there was left. To Heine, however, the sum of 6,000 marks, for reasons not entirely clear—he spoke of debts on the one hand and of a vacation in the country on the other—seemed to have acquired a talismanic power of its own; and since Heine was determined not to yield on the amount, he offered, by way of a compromise, to deliver an additional volume of miscellaneous writings for the same money. Sheer madness, for a man in his steadily deteriorating condition, but Mephistopheles Campe accepted the deal, and as always, he turned out to be the winner.

And so, in the spring of 1854, Heine whipped himself into another spurt of frantic activity which in the circumstances must have seemed little short of miraculous to all concerned. He kept two secretaries busy throughout most of the day, and it soon transpired that *Lutezia*, because of the new material he kept adding in order to overcome Campe's objections to "warmed-over news," would require a double volume. But it was the new prose and poetry of the first volume—first of what eventually came out as an inordinately expensive three-volume luxury edition—which along with a number of poems written subsequently and published after his death constitute Heine's literary testament. Strikingly different in tone and content for the most part, they mark the vast distance he had traveled, both as a poet and as a human being. He had shrunk into authenticity.

•

Intrepid, obsessed, either racked by pain or slowed by massive doses of opium, he still managed to tackle the task with great zest and efficiency, complaining all along that it had come at the wrong time because it interrupted him in the writing of his *Memoirs*, to which he was anxious to get back as soon as possible. Meanwhile, however, he would enclose a prose segment entitled "Confessions" in the manuscript for the first volume, "some eight to ten signatures," he wrote to Campe, "a piece that will please you very much because it constitutes, so to speak, the precursor to my *Memoirs*, which, however, will be written in a more popular and even much more picturesque style."

On March 10 he shipped all the manuscript material for the first volume off to Hamburg, understandably eager to have Campe's reaction as soon as possible. And once again he fell victim to one of those power games which the publisher apparently found both useful and irresistible and in which the depth of his manifestly pathological cruelty came into full play. When, two weeks later, Heine still had had no word from him, not even the mere acknowledgment of having received what in the days before typewriters and copiers was precious cargo indeed, he fairly begged Campe for an immediate reply or, in case of rejection, for the return of the manuscripts. "You know that because of my illness any delay of this sort puts me to a most cruel test . . . It is totally irresponsible on your part, the way you spoil my joy in my work, whereas I am constantly concerned with promoting your interests . . . You are truly killing me with your petty chicanery; not a very smart idea."

By April 1, Heine was desperate enough to call for help from Count Hermann von Pückler-Muskau, a liberal German aristocrat and ardent admirer. Pückler, the author of five travel books, happened to be passing through Paris on his way back to Germany. Generous and impulsive, he immediately agreed to negotiate on Heine's behalf and offered to pay him the contested 6,000 marks at once out of his own pocket. Having himself consistently received advances of at least 10,000 marks—in which, as Heine quietly pointed out, the market value of the name no doubt played a certain role—he nonetheless fully expected to recoup the loan without much trouble. Heine gave him a power of attorney and asked Campe to turn the manuscript over to him.

Predictably, the publisher reacted like the stuck pig he resembled. Feigning innocent outrage, he indignantly declared he had simply been too busy to pay immediate attention to Heine—after all, he had many other things to worry about—and received one of those inexplicably abject apologies that Heine would never have sent to anyone else: "Your incomprehensible silence gave rise to all sorts of tormenting thoughts, but I had no right to express any insulting accusations so long as I did not know what had happened . . . You must not, however, forget that I am a poet and quite unable to imagine that someone would not immediately drop everything else in order to read my poems . . . I can hardly see anymore what I am writing, but it eases my heart to know that I am back on friendly terms with you. Heaven knows that I wish you and your family all the good fortune in the world. A quarrel with you would be pure poison for me."

After a good deal of back and forth, Campe finally agreed to pay the 6,000 marks, and Heine in turn obligated himself to furnish not two but three volumes instead, each of them about 320 pages; it meant that "I would have to torture myself another four to five weeks just to receive the 6,000 marks that I could have obtained from others without such misery."

Torture himself he did, especially since right after the agreement in May his health took another turn for the worse. "I am sick as a dog," he wrote to Campe, "and I really don't feel up to coping with your complaints . . . You also happen to be wrong as to the nature of *my* complaints about you; they don't concern money so much as matters of ambition and feelings. I don't want to be treated like a raw recruit. When you were here, and I offered to let you read the *Romanzero* before you bought it, you said to me: 'You can't write anything bad. All you have to do is give me a book and put your name on it.' That was the way it was between Cotta and Goethe, although the latter gave Cotta quite a few weak things. Goethe never paid any attention to his publisher's criticism. What have I given you since then that would justify your change of tone?"

Now that he had signed the contract, Campe was in a desperate hurry to get the books out as fast as possible. Heine's increasingly precarious health may have played a role in his calculations, although characteristically what he complained about was the excessive postage he had been forced to pay for the corrections of the *Romanzero*; this by way of urging Heine to make as few changes as possible in the galleys. The energy and enthusiasm with which Heine responded seem all but incredible, although a remark of his in a letter to the bookseller Michael Schloss probably reveals part of the secret: "I am now publishing three rather than two volumes with Campe, and the aggravations and literary labor are such that they almost make me forget my illness."

The other passion that could provide some distraction was a good fight, and in his quarrel with Giacomo Meyerbeer he seems quite definitely to have had justice on his side. In May of 1854 the Berlin Opera staged a ballet called *Satanella*, clearly based on Heine's *Faust* ballet, which the Opera had rejected five years earlier. Meyerbeer, né Jakob Liebmann Beer—a fact Heine never let him forget—had just been appointed Superintendent of Music to the King of Prussia and, as such, head of the Opera; he in fact as much as admitted the plagiarism in front of witnesses but refused to do anything about it. Heine demanded royalties and, failing to get an answer, gave Meyerbeer a three-day ultimatum *sui generis*: "No newspaper in France or Germany would print a full-length accusation such as the case merits. You are all-powerful. I only have my books in which to speak freely, frankly, and with an open heart, and I will have to make use of a set that Hoffmann & Campe is about to bring out in Hamburg, three volumes of miscellaneous writings. The first is already off the press and contains only a few innocuous remarks about you. The second has gone off to the printer and also mentions you merely in passing. Only the third volume is still in my hands, but I have to send it off within the next six or seven days as per contract, and this is why I am giving you three days to react . . . I am not going to be put off by a simple promise. I am too ill, too unhappy, too furious to fall for any tricks. With the respect I have always reserved for your genius if not for your heart, I am . . ."

Meyerbeer failed to respond, and Heine hastily inserted a few predated scurrilous passages into the second volume of *Lutezia*. One of them, aside from demonstrating a peculiarly German addiction to anal humor, is also rather typical of the young Heine at his sophomoric worst, proof that even in the final stage of serene martyrdom he did not quite outgrow his adolescence:

The many fans and admirers of the admirable Maestro [Meyer-beer] worry about the way in which he spares no effort to assure the success of every new production of his genius and wastes his energy on the most minute details. His delicate, weak constitution is bound to suffer as a result. His nerves are morbidly tense, and his chronic abdominal ailment leads to frequent bouts of diarrhea. The honey of his spirit, which dribbles out of his musical masterpieces to give us joy, costs the Maestro himself some of the most horrible bellyaches. The last time I had the honor of seeing him I was shocked by his appearance. Seeing him reminded me of the God of Diarrhea in the Tartar folktale, which with uncanny humor tells how this grim-bellied Cacademon once bought six thousand chamber pots at the fair in Kazan for his personal use and made the potter a rich man. May the heavens grant the Maestro better health, and may he never forget what exalted interests are at stake in his self-preservation. What would become of his glory if death were suddenly to remove him from the stage of his triumphs?

And he goes on at tiresome length to denigrate Meyerbeer as a composer by praising his talent at public relations and proposes to fund claques and accommodating music critics out of the sizable estate to make sure that even after his death his works would be received in the manner to which they were accustomed.

•

In the best of times it was often difficult even for those who truly admired Heine's genius to reconcile it with his more problematic character traits—the flashes of paranoia, the unrestrained viciousness of his personal attacks on enemies or friends he felt had wronged him, his propensity to desecrate his pen—his sword, he called it, unchallenged in those pre-Freudian days—in exactly the kind of infantile temper tantrums of which the above is a not atypical example. What made it even harder to accept was his well-known but discreet generosity, his otherwise unfailing taste in matters literary, a sound dose of common sense, and the openness of spirit reflected in so much of his poetry and prose. His own explanation—for he was obviously not unaware of the problem—was the extreme sensitivity that made him the poet he was and which, as we have already seen, he blamed even for his physical decline. One is tempted to accept his judgment and forgo any in-depth posthumous analyses; the poet is human like the rest of mankind, only more so. The outward circumstances of his infancy, childhood, and adolescence ultimately did not differ significantly from those that shaped the lives of thousands of his contemporaries, German Jews from assimilated families in the post-Napoleonic period. What matters is the way they affected this particular life, and here his special gifts undoubtedly did play an important role; genius tends to exact a high price for its favors.

The entire month of July was an unending battle with proofs, corrections, deletions, and additions. In his eagerness to put the three-volume set on the market, Campe had the first volume printed in Halle and the other two in Kassel, the understanding being that Heine would be fully responsible only for Volume I, which contained the "Confessions," *The Gods in Exile*, and above all the new poems, while Campe himself would look after the two *Lutezia* volumes. Reinhardt did much of the spadework, but Heine's fanatical concern with the most minute details would let him delegate only so much of it, and his deteriorating eyesight coupled with Campe's ceaseless urging turned the job into a daily torture session. What made it worse was an uncomplimentary remark—not preserved—apparently scribbled on the margin of one of the galley proofs by some proofreader in the Halle printshop, which fed straight into Heine's paranoid fantasies about a conspiracy of printers determined to sabotage his work for political or religious reasons and spurred him on to even greater alertness. The work and the tension, combined with another relentless midsummer heat wave, brought him several times close to the brink, but death had become so familiar a presence in his life that he quite simply took it for granted. He warned Campe that he felt like a rabbit being chased by the hounds and was about to give out, but one gets the impression that in his heart of hearts he never really believed that he could die before the publication date, a conviction that may have helped keep him alive through a particularly stressful time.

Just to add to the stress, the house next door went up in flames, an almost total loss, and although their own building was ultimately spared, Heine's household had a moment of panic that reminded Heine that he carried no insurance and everyone else around him that there was no way of getting an invalid out of bed and down the five steep flights of stairs in a hurry. The incident may have contributed to the decision finally to leave the dreary dump on the rue d'Amsterdam; at the end of August they moved into what initially seemed a rather idyllic setup on the ground floor of a one-family house with access to a garden in Batignolles, now part of the Seventeenth Arrondissement but still quite rustic at the time. The idyll was short-lived. For a few weeks Heine enjoyed the garden, but they had a fight with the landlady, the apartment itself was dank and drafty, and he probably by now had absorbed enough of the French superstition about *les courants d'air* to blame them for a severe sore throat. How much he covered for Mathilde, who was deeply unhappy about the much greater distance from her favorite shops in the center of town, is anybody's guess, but at the beginning of November they moved once again, this time to a relatively upscale apartment house at 3, avenue Matignon, right off the Rond-Point of the Champs-Elysées, which now bears a plaque in Heine's memory.

Mathilde could hardly wish for a better location, presumably the main reason why she chose it.

Meanwhile, the frantic activity brought results, and the books came out in the middle of September, right on schedule, while at the same time the *Revue des Deux Mondes* of September 15 published a partial French version of the "Confessions," apparently translated by Heine himself. Though he bitterly resented their not having printed the text in its entirety, he felt triumphant. Numb, exhausted, sick unto death, but triumphant.

THE MOST CONSPICUOUS aspect of Heine's "Confessions" is their thoroughly unconfessional character. It may well be that asserting his belief in the existence of a personal God struck Heine as an act of contrition, but the tone of the essay—about 80 pages in the current editions—is anything but contrite. Five years in the mattress tomb clearly had done little to blunt his mordant sarcasm or moderate his righteous—often self-righteous—fury, and although he was writing on his deathbed, supposedly by way of making his peace with the world and the powers above, much of the piece is given over to polemics of one sort or another. Even the ostensible main theme, his conversion from atheism to whatever one wants to make of his faith, is made to sound considerably more amusing than convincing. For one thing, he once again exaggerates the Hegelian militancy of his younger self, whether for dramatic effect or because like many another aging ex-radical he saw himself in his recollections as far more radical than he had actually been. And for another, the God he found or to whom he returned seems *his* creation rather than the other way around. "No philosopher will ever again talk me into mistaking myself for a god. I am nothing but a poor human being, one moreover not entirely healthy and even very sick. In the circumstances it is a true blessing for me that there is someone up there in heaven to listen to me always whimpering and repeating the litany of my sufferings, especially after midnight, when Mathilde has retired for her well-earned rest. Thank God, in those hours I am not alone, and I can pray and bawl as much as I want without feeling ashamed, and

[*151*]

I can pour out my heart to the Almighty and confide certain things in Him that we normally tend to hide even from our own wives."

But the problem with Heine is that no statement of his can ever be taken at face value. "I don't know what he believes," the composer Ferdinand Hiller said about Heine, "but even though I believe that he knows it, I don't believe that he would so easily tell anybody the truth about it." The point is not that Heine was being deliberately duplicitous or mendacious. But he had early on learned to conceal his innermost feelings—to the extent to which he was himself aware of them—behind a smokescreen of self-irony, and in this particular instance one ends up not knowing whether he actually came to believe in some anthropomorphic God but made fun of his own faith because he was still too much the child of the Enlightenment not to be embarrassed by it, or whether this post-midnight father-confessor up in heaven was just another flight of his poetic fancy.

At any rate, whatever it is that the "Confessions" confess is served up pickled in acid, starting with another scurrilous attack on his old *bête noire* Mme de Staël. The daughter of the Swiss banker Jacques Necker, finance minister to Louis XVI, and for some years married to the Baron Staël-Holstein, Swedish ambassador to Paris, she ran one of the most brilliant literary salons in Paris, emigrated in 1792, and two years later began a stormy relationship with the novelist Benjamin Constant that ended in 1811, when she secretly married a scandalously younger Swiss officer. In 1797 she returned to Paris and published her first book, *De la Littérature considérée dans ses rapports avec les institutions sociales*, an at the time truly revolutionary view of literature as reflecting social conditions. She published two novels, *Delphine* in 1802 and *Corinne* in 1807, both of which qualify as early feminist writing, was exiled three times for her opposition to Napoleon (how gentle they were, the tyrants of old!), and in 1810 published *De l'Allemagne*, the work for which she is chiefly known. It was conceived as an encyclopedic disquisition on the unexplored territory beyond the Rhine, from its basic geography to its art, literature, philosophy, and religion, but in effect amounted to a comparison between France and Germany very much to the detriment of the former.

Heine had substantive and justifiable objections to the book on many accounts, most notably Mme de Staël's effusive exaltation of German Romanticism, which he saw as both source and symptom of reactionary obscurantism. He had raised these objections in two works of his own written in the 1830s—*The History of Religion and Philosophy in Germany* and *The Romantic School*, published jointly in French under the title of *De l'Allemagne* as a classic rejoinder to the Staël classic. But he detracts from the ideological thrust of his attack on German reaction—and by implication on the German past—by a view of women indistinguishable from that of the most retrograde of German philistines. Not that he was famous for undue tenderness toward his male adversaries; his gleeful exposure of Platen's homosexuality and of Börne's *ménage à trois* outraged even many of his friends. But in the case of Mme de Staël he was flogging a very dead lady indeed (she died in 1817) whom he had never known personally. Ignoring or dismissing her not inconsiderable intellectual achievements— among them the first comprehensive presentation of German literature and philosophy in French—he focused instead on her womanhood, or what he saw as such, "a tornado in women's clothes" sweeping through the peaceful German landscape in dogged pursuit of German luminaries and getting everything wrong. Her hatred of Napoleon he ascribes to his having rebuffed her sexual advances, and in the "Confessions" nearly two decades later he pursues the subject with a vigor curiously undiminished by either the passage of time or his own deplorable condition.

Hatred of the Emperor is the soul of her *De l'Allemagne* . . . Oh, these women! We must forgive them much, for they have much love, and many loves . . . Their hatred is basically only love that has changed horses . . . When they write, they keep one eye on the paper and the other on a man, and this is true of all women writers with the single exception of Countess Hahn-Hahn, who happens to only have one eye . . . I truly believe my friend Balzac was right when he once remarked, with a deep sigh, that *la femme est un être dangereux* . . . Yes, women are dangerous, though I should add that the beautiful ones aren't nearly as dangerous as are those who possess spiritual rather than physical assets. The latter are used to being courted, whereas the former have to lure men by flattering their vanity . . . I don't want to imply that Mme de Staël was ugly; but beauty is something else altogether.

And so on, at far greater length than would seem appropriate to a confessional. It seems impossible, in this farrago of wilted wit and wisdom, to disentangle the conventional prejudices of the age, shared by most men of whatever persuasion (and not only by men), from the fears and phobias specific to Heine, but it seems fairly evident that his devotion to the illiterate Mathilde, coupled with his marked hostility to emancipated women intellectuals, however common, was rooted somewhere in the realm of his private pathology.

The charge against Mme de Staël led into a series of sardonic portraits lampooning some of her more prominent disciples, a rogues' gallery that included the philosopher Friedrich von Schlegel, his wife, Dorothea "née Mendelssohn," the poet de La Motte Fouqué and the Vicomte de Chateaubriand. Heine once again demonstrated his unrivaled mastery of the poison pen, including an outrageous sense of the grotesque that in the circumstances can only be read as either morbid or heroic. But by the time the main theme finally manages to emerge—Heinrich Heine's Road to God— it has lost all its solemnity and much of its persuasiveness, which is, of course, merely a function of the author being himself. Heine even on his deathbed cannot be solemn, and as for persuasion, the one person with whom he carries on a never-ending argument is himself. It is this internal debate that constitutes the most interesting aspect of the "Confessions," illuminating as it does some of the feelings and attitudes at war within Heine and which, by putting him squarely on both sides of many an issue, in a strange way helped to enlarge his vision. Thus he boasts that "the emancipation of the people was the great task of our lives, and we struggled for it and suffered nameless misery, at home as in exile—but the clean, sensitive nature of the poet is repelled by any close personal contact with the people, and even more do we dread its caresses, may God save us from them. A great democrat once said that, had the King shaken his hand, he would immediately cleanse his hand by fire. In the same spirit I would say that I would wash my hands if the sovereign people had honored me with a handshake." Recalling his own turn away from atheism, he compares himself to Nebuchadnezzar, that once-proud King ultimately reduced to crawling like a beast and eating grass ("though it was probably salad," he remarks, in a typical aside), and enjoins his friend the Communist editor Arnold Ruge and "my even much more stubborn friend Marx," these "godless self-gods," to read the Book of Daniel themselves and draw the appropriate conclusions.

The "Confessions" are still intriguing in many ways, if tiresome in others, but they certainly cannot be taken seriously as an introspective account of metamorphosis and rebirth. This, I suspect, has as much to do with the medium as with the message. Heine's singular virtuosity as a master of German prose, the uncanny intimacy that so horrified Karl Kraus—"He loosened the bodice of the German language to the point where today any clerk can fondle her breasts"—was designed to dazzle rather than to probe. He skated across the surface like a champion, but when it came to exploring the lower depths, it took a poem.

Of the two other prose pieces included, along with the "Confessions," in the first volume of the *Miscellaneous Writings*, one—*The Gods in Exile*—has already been discussed. But another brief piece, "In Memory of Ludwig Marcus," is of more than passing interest. Written in 1844 as a eulogy of sorts to the Orientalist and Judaist Ludwig Marcus (or Markus), it contains the only substantive discussion of Heine's brief fling with the Society for the Science of Judaism back in 1822, of which Marcus was a fellow member at the time. He, too, emigrated for political reasons, taught German and English in Dijon, and eventually ended up living on Rothschild largesse in Paris, where he died insane in 1843 at the age of forty-five, a fate Heine linked to the existential situation of the exile in general. "So far as I know, no one is starving to death in a German dungeon. How many, on the other hand, have been carried off by poverty and privation in the free air, the airy freedom of liberal France?"

But his affectionate if condescending portrait of the multilingual polymath leads him into a rather devastating reevaluation of the once famous Verein, where "highly gifted and sincere men tried to save a long-lost cause; at best they succeeded in digging up the bones of earlier fighters on the battlefields of the past. The whole achievement of the Verein amounts to a few research projects in history, among which in particular Dr. Zunz's work about the Spanish Jews in the Middle Ages may count as one of the landmarks of higher criticism." The diagnosis is accurate enough, the main if unstated purpose of the Verein having been to ease the flight from Judaism for sentimentalists still clinging to vestigial traditions by transforming what used to be a living faith into a dead branch of science. But Heine, at the time of his most radical phase, went one step further. Like Marx, he saw modern anti-Semitism as class-based resentment of Jewish capitalism, bound to vanish with the "brotherhood of all the workers of the world, the wild armies of the proletariat, which will do away with the whole business of nationalities in order to pursue a common purpose throughout Europe, the realization of true democracy." Never before, nor ever after, did Heine mount such clattering Marxist platitudes. They were cut out of the original dispatch by the editor of the *Augsburger Allgemeine Zeitung*; Heine at first restored them for the *Miscellaneous Writings* but eventually thought better of it.

•

It would be naïve to maintain that a poet as facile and prolific as Heine could not have turned out a good deal of the trivial, the mediocre, and the altogether forgettable. But even in his minor poems he as a rule displays an inner discipline, a rigor of thought and language notably absent from his often far-ranging and discursive prose. In his poetry, he strove for the utmost economy of language. Every word was weighed, trimmed, measured, and neither irony nor wit was left to proliferate unchecked as so often happened in his prose. Heine's greatest poems achieve a tragic version of life starkly at odds with the *persona* of the playful ironist or paranoid polemicist that tends to dominate the prose.

The twenty-three poems included in the first volume of the *Miscellaneous Writings* mark its most memorable and enduring component, ultimately far more revealing in their pithy formulation than the self-conscious "Confessions." There is a new, intimate tone to the first five poems, an internal dialogue reflecting the tension between the will to live and the wish to die:

> *O Grab, du bist das Paradies*
> *Für pöbelscheue, zarte Ohren—*
> *Der Tod ist gut, doch besser wär's*
> *Die Mutter hätt uns nie geboren.*

> *(O tomb, you are the paradise*
> *For tender ears that cannot bear the mob*
> *Death may be good, but better yet*
> *If no mother had ever borne us.)*

> *Es blüht der Lenz. Im grünen Wald*
> *Der lustige Vogelsang erschallt,*
> *Und Mädchen und Blumen, sie lächeln jungfräulich—*
> *O schöne Welt, du bist abscheulich!*

> *(Spring has come. Happy birdsong fills the woods*
> *Girls and flowers smile their virgin smile*
> *O beautiful world, you are disgusting.)*

But after five poems centered on his own grim state of body and soul, Heine abruptly shifts the focus outward and in a brilliant outburst of social protest—social outrage, more precisely—pillories racism and Christian hypocrisy with venomous sarcasm and an icy eloquence that could and very well might have served as a model to the early Brecht. The growing conflict over slavery in the United States was much in the news at the time, and in 1854, when "The Slave Ship" was written, France had just outlawed slavery in all her colonies. Heine had always been extremely sensitive to the issue, but in this instance he succeeded in clearly focusing his rage and, with extraordinary control of both language and plot, wrote a poem which, along with "The Silesian Weavers," ranks among his very best, a masterpiece of its kind and, not incidentally, the first anti-racist poem in the German language.

Six hundred black slaves on a Dutch merchant ship bound for Rio de Janeiro are dying at a rate that would leave few of them alive on arrival. Having calculated that at least half must survive if they are to make a profit, the supercargo and the ship's physician postulate melancholy as the cause of the excess mortality and force the chained slaves, for the sake of their health, to participate every night in a *danse macabre* on deck, with the whip beating the rhythm, the corpses fed to the sharks, while the pious Mynheer van Kock stands by the foremast praying to his God:

> "Um Christi willen verschone, o Herr,
> Das Leben der schwarzen Sünder!
> Erzürnten sie dich, so weisst du ja,
> Sie sind so dumm wie die Rinder.

> "Verschone ihr Leben um Christi will'n,
> Der für uns alle gestorben!
> Denn bleiben mir nicht dreihundert Stück,
> So ist mein Geschäft verdorben."

> ("For Jesus' sake, O Lord, spare these
> Black sinners' lives here below!
> If they offended you, after all
> They're just dumb cattle, you know.

> *"Oh, spare their lives for Jesus' sake*
> *Who did not die in vain!*
> *For if I don't keep three hundred head*
> *My business is down the drain."*

Several of the poems dramatize old wounds, still bleeding or else artificially kept open, rather like the open sores on his back through which he received his opium. In "Die Wahlverlobten" ("The Elective Betrothed") he for the last time settles the score with the long since mythical beloved who once rejected him, her beauty now dust and ashes because beauty is mortal, whereas poets never quite die but live on in the fairyland of poetry: *Leb wohl auf ewig, schöne Leiche.* (Farewell forever, beautiful corpse.) "Affrontenburg" ("Castle of Insults") is an allegorical curse upon Uncle Salomon's mansion, scene of so many of his early humiliations. And, as always to the very end, Heine could not resist lampooning his enemies.

Two of his targets, the poet Georg Herwegh and the liberal publicist Jakob Venedy, don't quite seem to warrant the heavy ammunition, but in "Erinnerungen aus Krähwinkels Schreckenstagen" ("Recollections of the Days of Terror in Podunk") he demonstrates that when duly aroused—and the wave of reactionary spirit in Germany still somehow had the power to upset him—he had lost none of his old bite and vigor:

> *Ausländer, Fremde sind es meist,*
> *Die unter uns gesät den Geist*
> *Der Rebellion. Dergleichen Sünder,*
> *Gottlob! Sind selten Landeskinder.*
>
> *Wer auf der Strasse räsonniert,*
> *Wird unverzüglich füsiliert*

*Das Räsonnieren durch Gebärden*
*Soll gleichfalls hart bestrafet werden.*

*Vertrauet eurem Magistrat,*
*Der fromm und liebend schützt den Staat*
*Durch huldreich hochwohlweises Walten;*
*Euch ziemt es, stets das Maul zu halten.*

(*It was mostly foreigners, strangers who sowed the spirit of re-*
*bellion among us. Such sinners, thank God, are seldom natives.*

*Whosoever argues in the street will be shot at once. Arguing by*
*gesture will also be punished severely.*

*Have confidence in your magistrate, who with great love and*
*wisdom protects the state. As far as you are concerned, your job*
*is to keep your trap shut.*)

The epilogue catches the spirit of the whole:

*Unser Grab erwärmt der Ruhm.*
*Torenworte! Narrentum!*
*Eine bessere Wärme gibt*
*Eine Kuhmagd die verliebt*
*Uns mit dicken Lippen küsst*
*Und beträchtlich riecht nach Mist . . .*

(*Fame warms our grave?*
*What nonsense.*
*A far better sort of warmth gives the lovelorn milkmaid*
*Who kisses us with her fat lips*
*And stinks of manure.*)

[*161*]

The fragment of the "Confessions" published in the September issue of the *Revue des Deux Mondes* in advance of the German publication was instantly pounced upon by the literary pirates and, badly retranslated, appeared in the *Augsburger Allgemeine Zeitung* along with a rather scurrilous commentary. Heine immediately broke off all relations with his former paper and asked Campe to take legal action against it, but finally settled for a public protest.

Unfortunately the comments in the *Allgemeine* merely anticipated similar critical reactions to the *Miscellaneous Writings* in most of the German press. A quarter of a century had passed since Heine had left the country; the literary as well as the political scene had undergone some drastic changes. His former audience of pre-'48 liberals was gone, sapped by old age and death or swamped by the tide of reaction that swept the country. The men now setting the tone in the realm of culture were the ones who knew how to navigate that tide, and they had no use for Heine. Not that all of their critical comments were necessarily far-fetched or unfair; Heine's persistent egocentricity and the often quite unwarranted virulence of his personal attacks alienated many of his readers, and despite his own rather exalted ideas about their lasting interest, the two *Lutezia* volumes covering Paris in the early forties failed to catch on in the Germany of the fifties. Added to that was the ambiguity of Heine's politics, the politics of a man who knows what he is against but seldom what he is for, and who finds it impossible to commit himself uncritically to any cause. He still liked to view himself as a revolutionary, but no one else took him seriously in that role, and by simultaneously predicting and deploring the victory of Communism, he neatly placed himself between the lines, drawing fire from both sides.

In the circumstances, it seemed particularly unwise on Campe's part to price the set at an astronomical six talers, the equivalent today of anywhere between two and three hundred dollars. Heine complained bitterly about it, to no avail. Publishers à la Campe—a species now extinct—used to be guided by hunches, whims, and mysterious voices from inside their head. Some such persuaded Campe not only to price himself practically out of the market but also to print what for his day was a huge first edition of 3,500 copies. There never was a second, as compared to the French version, which had gone through no less than nine editions by 1871.

But even taking into account all the adverse circumstances that conspired against him, it became apparent that Heine had begun to outlive his reputation, at least in Germany, and that he was about to undergo that inevitable eclipse that for all but a handful of the chosen ends in oblivion.

THE EFFORT involved in publishing the *Miscellaneous Writings* brought Heine once again to the brink of death. In October 1854 he came down with a severe throat infection that he blamed on the dank apartment in Batignolles and that kept him, or should have kept him, from even dictating letters. In addition, he had to undergo the surgical removal of a cyst in his back. That in eight years of near-complete paralysis and immobilization in a recumbent position, without the benefit of antibiotics, air conditioning, and even rudimentary asepsis he successfully escaped pneumonia or any of the other infectious diseases which a century ago tended to terminate such lingering invalidism in short order defies every rule of probability, and modern medical opinion has not really come up with a cogent explanation, except for paying lip service to the occasional triumph of mind over matter.

At the beginning of November his spirits lifted considerably with the move to what finally, late in the day, turned out to be an apartment suitable from every point of view. It was bright and airy, right off the Champs-Elysées, and from his shaded balcony off a room twice the size of his previous one Heine had a view of the Rond-Point. Adolf Stahr, who saw him right after the move (and who with compulsive pedantry counted 105 stairs from the street to Heine's fifth-floor apartment), quotes him as saying how happy he initially was "after so many years to see the world again with half my eye, and yet it was so little. I had borrowed my wife's binoculars and with incredible pleasure watched a pastry baker offer his wares to two ladies in crinolines, and a little dog standing on three legs by a tree next to them and relieving himself. At that point I put away the binoculars. I didn't want to see anything anymore. Because I envied the dog."

The German reception of the *Miscellaneous Writings* naturally depressed him, but he tended to regard book reviewing in Germany as largely a matter of political conspiracies and reproached Campe for "no longer having a single person in the German literary establishment on whose sympathies you can count when it comes to launching a new book of mine." Although his inveterate paranoia certainly played into this view, it was far from unrealistic, and while book reviewing is everywhere linked to literary and other kinds of politics, the corruption in Germany to this day far outpaces that in most other countries.

The enthusiastic acclaim that greeted Taillandier's translation of some of the "Lazarus" poems in France made up to some extent for the German fiasco and persuaded Heine to fling himself straightway into another of those backbreaking chores that seemed to help him keep the "evil Thanatos" at bay. He signed a contract with his French publisher, Michel Lévy frères, for the French version of *Lutosia*, and agreed to undertake the translation himself. As we know, in the end it was largely the work of his secretary Reinhardt, but he himself still put in some five to seven hours daily editing, adding, and revising, far more than he thought was warranted, because "the French translation of this book, like all the French editions of my books, brings in very little money. They chiefly serve to advertise my name. Whoever has not earned a great, an immense reputation in France cannot boast of a European reputation."

The impending release of the French edition of *Lutezia* also called for some defensive footwork. As was to be expected, Heine in his old newspaper dispatches had treated a good many people in French public life with the contempt he thought they deserved, his attacks on them ranging from barbed comments to out-and-out character assassination. Most of them had either disappeared from the scene or were not important enough to worry about. But Thiers and Guizot, both ministers under Louis Philippe and as such frequent targets of Heine's less than complimentary remarks, were once again powerful figures under the new regime, and it would not do to have them take offense. In a couple of rather fulsome letters he assured them that from his point of view the period covered in *Lutezia* was dominated by three men—Louis Philippe, Thiers, and Guizot, and that regardless of occasional criticism on his part— unavoidable when writing for a German newspaper—these three were the heroes of his book. Both men acknowledged his letters with the sort of polite notes that the French can turn out without even engaging the brain; they were obviously not overly worried about the threat to their reputation.

A much more delicate problem presented itself in relation to the Rothschilds. Betty, the German-born wife of James de Rothschild, head of the Paris branch, was one of Heine's ardent admirers, and he had repeatedly been a guest at their house, a fact that did not prevent him from occasionally asking for what in effect amounted to a handout, not in cash but in shares; with every new issue the baron always made it a practice to set aside a certain number for charitable purposes. As a rule he proved generous, and Heine's treatment of him in *Lutezia* was on the whole respectfully sympathetic. Nevertheless, as the baron also loomed as a very quiet but very large presence in French politics behind the scenes, he of necessity had received a great deal of attention, and Heine felt that some of the remarks about him he was now resurrecting might lend themselves to misinterpretation. He sent the baron's wife a dedicatory copy of the book and enclosed a letter warning her that "there may be certain parts in it where, when speaking of the baron, my language may not quite reflect the devotion one owes a patron . . . In essence I don't believe myself guilty of any lack of tact. If the baron occasionally honored me by calling me his friend, I was never so immodest as to take this for more than an amiable *courtoisie* . . . The moments I spent in his company belong to my most pleasant and joyful memories."

Two months later, apparently reassured, he drafted a letter to James de Rothschild that must be considered a minor masterpiece of *shnorrery*:

Dear Baron, knowing that you are surely looking for a delicate way of easing my situation by improving my finances, I would like to meet you halfway by asking you to have me participate for as large a number of shares as possible in the great new loan offering of 500 million. I can hear you reply that my participation does not require your intervention, since the subscription is open to any-one. This, of course, is true. But I have the honor to point out that a truly substantial gain requires a large investment and the immediate outlay of a considerable amount, which would cause me serious financial embarrassment I would escape this embar-rassment if you, my dear Baron, made the deposit on my behalf. Furthermore, since I am unable to attend the stock exchange sessions and could not gauge the right moment to prevent a pos-sible loss by timely divestment, I would avoid this danger by entrusting this operation to the great financier, who is bound always to win in this sort of game. Let me sum up: I neither want to invest a penny nor risk a penny, and what I want to participate in is not so much the loan but your share of the profit in it . . . I am sick as a dog, I work like a horse, and I am poor like a church-mouse . . . I had the pleasure of hearing from Mme the Baroness that given your sense of humor I do not need to worry about having offended you, which would have disturbed me very much.

In a similar vein he requested a gift of 100 shares of the new Society for Austrian Rails and Mines from the bank of Emile Pereire so as to allow him one year of uninterrupted work on his *Memoirs* rather than waste his time in pointless labor and was extremely angry when Pereire fobbed him off with a mere twenty shares. None of this was, of course, especially unusual in an era in which support for the arts still had to rely entirely on private patronage and in which neither public funding nor professional grant collectors had yet made their appearance.

Furthermore, Heine in the last few years of his life and within his limited means made a number of conservative investments, all of them so far as can be determined in railroad stock, which had nowhere to go but up, given the furious expansion of the rail net throughout Europe. Clearly he worried a great deal about Mathilde's future—but one also gets the impression that he derived a certain sporting satisfaction from this first gingerly contact with the poisoned wellsprings of capitalism.

·

At dawn on January 26, 1855, the body of Gérard de Nerval was found hanging from a lamppost in the rue de la Vieille Lanterne. He was forty-six years old.

Born Gérard Labrunie, the son of a doctor in the Napoleonic armies, he qualified as the quintessential *poète maudit* long before the genus as such received official recognition. He was from the very beginning a creature entirely of intuition and inspiration, resisting ordinary reason with that gentle manner that made him so beloved a character among the lower depths of *la Bohème*; thus, although his German was scarcely more than rudimentary, he at the age of twenty produced a French translation of Goethe's *Faust* which Goethe himself praised as superb. In 1831 he fell in love, came under the spell of, or conceived an unconsummated obsession for, Jenny Colon, a fickle two-bit actress whose sole claim to immortality resides in her once having been the object of Nerval's abiding passion. The superficial parallels between this lovingly nurtured wound and his own bittersweet fantasy of youthful love inspired countless jokes on Heine's part, but in this instance even he steered clear of anything potentially hurtful. He grew extremely fond of Gérard, probably the closest friend he ever made among the French. For all their outward differences, they seemed linked in a strange affinity at the poetic and no doubt at the emotional level as well, which may account for the uncanny perfection with which Nerval's translations capture the spirit of the original. After Nerval's first breakdown in 1841, relations with him became increasingly difficult, but although in and out of asylums and largely living in the street, he wrote several haunting works he called *super-naturalistes* and which in due course came to be claimed by both the Symbolists and the Surrealists.

His suicide thus came as a profound shock to Heine at a moment when he was particularly vulnerable. In the preface to *Poèmes et Légendes*, a collection of his poetry in translation published in the spring of 1855, he for once dispensed with the usual ironic detachment and paid a straightforward and palpably heartfelt tribute to his friend:

I could not resist the painful pleasure of reprinting in this book the gracious pages with which my late friend Gérard de Nerval prefaced the "Intermezzo" and "North Sea." And it is with the most profound emotion that I recall our evenings together in March 1848, when the good and gentle Gérard came every day to see me in my lair at the Barrière de la Santé to work quietly with me on the translation of my peaceful German dreams, while all around us raged the passions of politics and the old world collapsed with an incredible roar . . . Gérard, even in his lucid days, was always easily distracted, and rather too late to do anything about it, I discovered that he had lost seven poems of the "North Sea" series. I left the gap so as not to destroy the harmony of color and rhythm by interspersing the rough products of my own pen. Gérard's diction flowed with an inimitable purity that could be likened only to the incomparable gentleness of his soul. He truly was more soul than man, I would say the soul of an angel, however banal the expression. It was a soul essentially empathic, and without knowing much about the German language, Gérard had a better feel for the sense of a German poem than did those who had studied the language all their lives. He was a great artist . . . and yet he had none of the artist's egotism. He was all childlike candor, delicate sensitivity. He was good, he loved everybody, he envied no one. He never hurt a fly and shrugged his shoulders if a dog bit him. And in spite of all these qualities my friend Gérard ended up in the little street of the Vielle Lanterne.

Poverty was not the cause of this sinister event, but neither did it stop him. The fact is that at the fatal hour the unfortunate man did not even have a reasonably clean and heated room at his disposal where he could have . . .

Poor child. You well deserve the tears spilled on your behalf, and I cannot contain my own in writing these lines. Yet your earthly sufferings are over, whereas those of your collaborator of the Barrière de la Santé still continue. But don't you feel too sorry for me, dear reader; the day may not be too far off when you will need all your pity for yourself. Do you have any idea how you may end up someday?

•

In the winter of 1854–55, Heine's condition took a decided turn for the worse. He still managed to accomplish a great deal of work—poems, translations, new prefaces, and editorial work on the forthcoming French editions that were rolling off the presses at a fast pace, in addition to at least 130 letters written in the thirteen months between January and his death the following year. But his forces were visibly giving out, there were weeks when he felt absolutely incapable of attending to any of the routine chores and when his sole comfort was the poems composed in the dead of night. A serious throat ailment added a racking cough to his other torments and made even prolonged conversation increasingly difficult, a particularly nasty blow in that the 1855 Paris World's Fair brought thousands of visitors from Germany, among them many with whom he was eager to talk. Fanny Lewald, who saw him in the spring, reports that for the first time she sensed a note of despair: "Imagine that I, who love art, have not seen a picture in the past seven years. Altogether, who can imagine my situation? The guiding principle of my existence is the word 'nevermore.' Did you ever realize what a terrible word that is? Never walk again. Never see again. Nevermore. It approaches like a heavy steamroller and flattens everything in its way—until finally we ourselves end up under it, and the nevermore is complete." Fanny Lewald suggested spiritual advice, but her suggestion was quietly ignored.

Early in June Heine learned that his brother Gustav planned to visit the fair and implored him to stop off in Hamburg on the way and bring along their sister Charlotte, "whom, without your authoritative intervention, they would never permit to come here by herself. I was so sick all winter that I looked forward to the end and was often about to write to Lottchen and ask her to come here so we could talk once more, which would be a great comfort to me on my voyage to eternity. It will not cost her a sou. My wife already has a room all prepared for her, and she will be no burden to you, either, since afterwards I'll send her back to Hamburg, postage paid. Everything is so easy now, and she is no child anymore. She can certainly take the train back to Hamburg by herself . . . P.S.: I am very sick, dear brother, and I plead with you to insist that Lottchen at least come here in the course of the summer."

And then, a few weeks later, in the middle of June, the Goddess of Poetry or some higher power addicted to hearts and flowers, violins and Hollywood sunsets arranged for an on the face of it quite improbable final chapter.

THERE WAS SOMETHING vaguely mysterious about the way she turned up in the avenue Matignon on the morning of June 19, 1855. But then, the faint odor of mystery and mystification trailed her all her life, and it was not until long after her death that some of the questions were at least tentatively answered.

At the time she went under the name of Elise Krinitz, and as she told the story many years later, a composer friend in Vienna who shared her admiration of Heine had set some of his poems to music and asked her, since she was headed for Paris, to deliver the score to the poet personally. She did so, "and just as I was about to leave, a shrill bell was being rung in the next room, and a rather peremptory voice asked me to come in. I opened the door and in the sudden darkness inside bumped into a wall screen. Behind it, on a rather low pallet, lay a sick, half-blind man who looked considerably younger than his age and whose features excited an uncanny fascination: the head of Christ, with a face animated by the smile of a Mephistopheles. He took my hand and expressed his joy at seeing someone from 'down there' . . . In the face of death one fast becomes friends, and when I was leaving, Heine gave me a book and asked me to come and see him again. I took the invitation for mere routine politeness and did not take him up on it. But then the invitation was repeated in writing, and the reproach which accompanied it both upset and flattered me."

This, presumably, was more or less how it happened, although for reasons best known to herself she failed to inform either Heine or posterity that, among many other things, she had for two years been the lover of Heine's close friend Alfred Meissner. Still, to give her the benefit of the doubt she so richly deserves, it may have been a certain delicacy of feeling, a blessed sense of compassion that silenced her rather than any devious schemes; it can have taken no great wisdom of the heart for her to be aware of Heine's troubled emotions, and he was in any case way beyond hiding them. The famous *coup de foudre*, one last rebellion of Eros against Thanatos. Futile as always, and in this instance more like a drowning man clutching at a dream.

Still, for one brief moment it made life seem possible once more.

The following day he sent her a note:

My dear amiable and charming person,
I greatly regret having been able to see you but for a few moments. You made an extremely favorable impression, and I am longing for the pleasure of seeing you again. If possible, come tomorrow, or in any case whenever your time permits. Announce yourself as last time. I am ready to receive you at any hour. The best time for me would be from 4 p.m. until as late as you want. Despite my eye trouble I am writing to you in my own hand, because at the moment I don't have a confidential secretary. I have lots of trouble on my plate and am suffering a great deal. I don't know why your kind sympathy seems to do me so much good and why I want to imagine, superstitious as I am, that a good fairy is visiting me in a sad hour. It was the right hour. Or are you a bad fairy? I must find out soon.

•

Her name at birth is unknown to this day, but it is now generally believed that she was born in Prague in 1828, the illegitimate daughter of a Count Nostitz, given up for adoption to a German family named Krinitz who came to live in Paris, where she grew up bilingual. Her legal name was Elise Krinitz, but she was so adept at —or addicted to— romantic obfuscation that for a long time Meissner knew her only as Margot. There is the story of an early marriage that ended when her brute of a husband had her forcibly committed to an English insane asylum, a traumatic interlude which for some months rendered her aphasic. Not altogether inconceivable, but then again quite possibly the product of an easily overheated imagination. At any rate, having regained her speech and eventually her freedom, she returned to Paris, where, at the age of twenty-seven, she had her fateful meeting with Heine. Demure, petite, with dreamy, delicate features, she possessed both the experience and the malleability to adapt with great skill to the role the dying poet had assigned to her, which involved no real hardship, since she quite obviously adored him. But as she was to prove later on in life, there was a solid core to her. In 1858, rebaptized or reborn as Camille Selden, she became the mistress of the fiercely anti-romantic French critic and historian Hippolyte Taine and, in addition to a novel, produced several studies of German literature as well as a French translation of Goethe's *Elective Affinities*. Ditched by Taine after a ten-year relationship, she obtained a teaching post in a girls' school in Rouen and in 1884 published her recollections of Heine, *Les Derniers jours de H. Heine*. Despite lapses into sentimentality, the book on the whole is remarkably sensible and informative, a tribute to the author's intelligence and a major source for Heine's final days if read with the creative skepticism all such memoirs call for. Thus she left us a graphic description of the Heine household in 1855 which generally checks with other independent sources:

At a time when most artists tried to settle in at least a comfortable if not elegant home, it struck me as particularly strange to find Heine in rooms wholly devoid of either elegance or comfort, with furniture dating from an era long since gone. I wondered what accounted for it, whether it was mere carelessness, a disdain for external things, or if the household was perhaps unduly constrained by the need for strict economy?

When I saw him for the first time, Heine lived near the Champs-Elysées on the fifth floor of a house on the avenue Matignon . . . The furniture in the sickroom consisted of a low pallet behind a screen, a few chairs, and a desk. There was no trace of a woman's touch in these arrangements . . . I had imagined Frau Heine as an elegant, delicate figure with pale, interesting features and large, enigmatic eyes. Instead, what I met was a brown-haired, fairly hefty lady who looked smugly satisfied and, to judge from her healthy color, spent a good deal of time out-of-doors. It was rather painful to see this picture of health and life next to the pale martyr . . . and yet this sick man, tied to life by only the thinnest of threads, was still slaving away for his wife's daily bread and for her beautiful dresses. No eyewitness will buy the claptrap of biographers spouting nonsense about a man having been too much in love to curb his wife's extravagance. To turn into an idyll what the poet himself never presented as such would be to shortchange the truth, which in this instance can only honor his memory.

On some points the author's objectivity even at the distance of nearly thirty years may be subject to doubt. Mathilde took an instant dislike to the young, fresh-faced intruder at ease in both German and French and resented the intimacy that quickly developed between her and Heine. But where as a rule she used to make a great show of her jealousy, whether warranted or not, she in this instance forwent her habitual temper tantrums and widely if grudgingly tolerated the rival presence. She drew the line, however, at inviting her to dinner or even letting her eat at the table along with the rest of the household, even though Heine repeatedly asked her to; she simply would not break bread with "that woman."

Mouche was the name Heine gave her, inspired by the pattern on her seal ring, and of all her various aliases that is the one under which she attained a measure of immortality. "My sweetest *fine mouche*," he wrote in mid-July, less than a month after their first meeting. "Or should I name you after the scent of your letter rather than the emblem on your seal ring? In that case I would have to call you the loveliest muskrat. I had your letter the day before yesterday. The *pattes de mouche* keep swarming in my head and perhaps also in my heart. Thank you for all the love you're devoting to me. The poems are very beautiful, and on that score I can only repeat what I already told you. I, too, am very much looking forward to seeing you soon and to *poser une empreinte vivante sur les traits suaves et quelque peu souabes*—If only I were still a man, this phrase would take a less platonic turn. But I am now merely a ghost, which may perhaps suit you but which I find rather distressing. The French edition of my poems has appeared and is making waves . . . Yes, I am looking forward to seeing you again, *fine mouche de mon âme*. Loveliest of muskrats, but soft like an Angora cat, my favorite breed. I used to like tiger cats, but they are too dangerous, the *empreintes vivantes* they used to leave in my face were not terribly pleasant. I am still in a bad state, constant cramps and anger. Anger at my condition, which is hopeless. A dead man thirsting for the greatest of life's pleasures. Horrible. Farewell. May the spa refresh and restore you."

·

She had entered his life just when he had begun to let go of it. *"Quelque moribond qu'on soit,"* he had written two years earlier, *"l'homme doit faire son devoir de vivant jusqu'au dernier moment."* But the duties had become increasingly onerous, and the stifling heat of midsummer did not make things any easier for him. The first French edition of *Lutezia* came out in June. For the Germans, these articles had been yesterday's news from another country; for the French they were their own recent history and generated considerable excitement. Yet even this failed to do much for his mood. "The success of *Lutezia*, main topic of conversation in Paris for the past two weeks, has scared me very much. To speak the truth is a dangerous business, especially for a sick man who needs his rest. I therefore, while I am still alive, shall make it a point not to publish any more books written with the same freedom and absolute truthfulness. What I have to say about our contemporary society will appear someday in my posthumous *Memoirs*."

The appearance of a worshipful young admirer by his bedside came just in time to revive the flagging will to live. That he instantly fell in love with her was a sign of some residual glow in the embers; what must have come as something of a shock to him, especially given his attitude toward women, was the discovery that she not only had a mind of her own but also a fairly good education, and when Zichlinsky, his new secretary, repeatedly left him in the lurch, he began, as she somewhat coyly put it, "to make use of the small talents of his Mouche." Despite a few minor problems with the intricacies of German grammar and—what Heine found especially provoking—with the calligraphy of German capital letters, she not only proved a rather capable bilingual secretary but also began to translate some of his poems, one of which appeared in the *Revue des Deux Mondes* and marked her literary debut.

But whatever the emotional gratification, it could no longer offset the proliferation of physical symptoms. Pain-racked nights or incapacitating migraine headaches lasting for days on end forced him more and more often to cancel meetings with the Mouche or to refuse to receive visitors. He drafted a Last Will and Testament in July which, however unwise some of its stipulations, seems clearly to contradict the Mouche's impression of his marriage. Mathilde was appointed universal legatee, with full rights to all property present and future, most particularly those deriving from the exploitation of the literary estate.

"I hereby formally declare that it is not only as my legitimate spouse that I appoint Mathilde Crescence Heine née Mirat my sole heir but also as testimony of my affection and gratitude. I by this act want to give proof of my friendship to the woman who for twenty years has been my beloved and faithful companion in the vicissitudes of exile and who has cared for me with solid devotion during the terrible years of this cruel and capricious illness to which I am succumbing. I request my wife to take charge of all my papers and correspondence immediately upon my death and to dispose of them in accordance with my written or oral instructions." (The testament was never executed, leaving the November 1851 will as the final valid one.)

Whenever he was physically able to, he continued to work on the French edition of his Collected Works, driven by an avowed need to earn money that had become something of an obsession. But as he wrote to his brother, he had a fixed income of only 12,000 francs a year while needing a minimum of 24,000 because of his illness, so that he could not possibly get along without the royalties from his writings in Germany and in France, "where they have been having a miraculous success. I am also negotiating with Campe. He is still furious about the unauthorized publication of my works in America, but they have furthered my reputation to such an extent that an American literary critic will be giving lectures about me in New York and in Albany, an honor which thus far no living poet has ever received." The lectures cannot be confirmed, but an unauthorized edition of *Pictures of Travel* translated by one Leland was published in Philadelphia in 1855, followed in 1856 by Volumes I and II of a Collected Edition.

Even his quarrels pursued him to the end. Or he them. The final one involved an obscure Austrian composer named Joseph Dessauer, whom Heine considered a creature of Meyerbeer and whom, in one of the passages added to *Lutezia* but supposedly written years earlier, he accused of having bragged about an affair with George Sand. Dessauer countered by accusing Heine of once having tried to extort 500 francs from him for a favorable review; George Sand publicly exonerated Dessauer; Heine saw a plot by Meyerbeer acting in concert with the enemies within his own family; brother Gustav jumped in with his two flat feet and stirred up matters further; and in the end, the case went to court after Heine's death. The final disposition is unknown, but since no one could ever quite figure out what it was about in the first place, this hardly matters.

With the arrival of fall Heine grew increasingly anxious about seeing his sister once more. Since brother Gustav came with the package, he urged him in October to get moving lest he be too late. "I am unfortunately very, very ill. The end is near. And yet I'll be terribly happy to see the two of you, although I'm afraid the trip won't be very amusing for you . . . But even though you won't have much fun, it should still make you feel better to have seen me once more before I move on. My enemies can't hurt me much, I am used to their lies, but my friends were the ones that made my life miserable. Prudence demands that I say nothing about the extent to which my physical condition prevents me from working."

•

Charlotte Emden and Gustav Heine arrived in Paris on November 4. It was understood to be a final goodbye, hence a highly emotional occasion for all concerned, yet each came away with a rather different impression in the end. There is first of all the so-to-speak official account of the meeting in the clanking prose of the self-important Baron Gustav von Heine-Geldern, whose monumental obtuseness could almost lead one to wonder about the exact nature of the genetic link with his brother:

I journeyed to Paris via Hamburg, since my brother had expressed the wish to see our there residing sister Charlotte Emden one more time . . . We arrived in Paris at midnight, hence had to postpone the visit for the following morning. It was indeed a horrible reunion. The poor patient lay there just as paralyzed as I had left him four years earlier. Charlotte, despite my attempt to prepare her, got so upset that she was sick for several days . . . Once Charlotte left the sickroom, Harry wanted to talk business; he had really summoned me to Paris to talk about his estate . . . which he wanted me to administer after his death. I must frankly confess that when I thought of his latest works and listened to him talk without the slightest regard for the most fundamental realities of life, I sometimes wondered if it was really my brother Harry talking to me. Seven years of bodily misery had alienated him from the external world, he seemed totally unfamiliar with the routine of ordinary life on this planet. It was a whole new world that he had created for himself on his sickbed.

Charlotte's recollections, on the other hand, reflect genuine sisterly love, even though they may have been somewhat prettified for the benefit of posterity:

As I bent over his bed, he clasped me in his arms for a long time without saying a word, then finally leaned his head against my shoulder and shook hands with his brother. His joy at seeing me was indescribable, and I was not allowed to leave his bedside from morning to night except for meals. After all I had heard about my brother's illness, I was afraid that the first sight of him would upset me profoundly, but since I saw only the head, which was of a miraculous, serene beauty, I was able to abandon myself completely to the first joy of the reunion. But when, in the afternoon, the nurse carried my brother to the couch to make the bed and I saw the shriveled body with the lifeless legs, I had to mobilize all my strength to cope with this terrible sight . . . Mathilde got along with me very well, not so with Gustav, who spoke no French, could not communicate with her, and, moreover, considered his brother's love match a disaster and the cause of all his suffering . . . I was rather glad when Gustav returned to Vienna by himself . . .

My brother told me about a pleasant, strangely gifted young woman, a German who combined French esprit with German sentiment . . . so well versed in French that he was able to let her read the proofs of his works, momentarily somewhat indisposed but soon to show up again, and he was curious as to my impression of her. Mouche, as he called her . . . was in fact a lovely, youthful apparition whom I came to like a great deal during my brief stay. Of medium height, attractive rather than beautiful, a delicate face framed by brown curls, mischievous eyes, a snubnose, and a small mouth with pearly teeth. There was something uncommonly graceful about all her movements . . . Mouche visited my brother for several hours every day, and unfortunately his affection for the lively little one aroused a morbid degree of jealousy in Mathilde, which ended in open animosity. Despite her husband's request, Mathilde stubbornly refused to let the girl dine with him, she barely responded to her friendly greetings and upon her arrival left the sickroom immediately . . .

At the beginning of December I was suddenly informed of my children's illness and decided to return to Hamburg. I asked Dr. Gruby what he thought of my brother's condition and was given the comforting news that, barring some unforeseen complication, he could still live another two or three years.

Camille Selden in her memoirs barely mentions the meeting but also stresses the instant friendship between herself and Charlotte. The only contemporary testimony is that of Heine himself in a letter to her dated Saturday, November 10, 1855, which sums up the situation in one brief marginal comment: "Sweetest Person, I have a terrible headache today and will probably have to live with its afterbirth tomorrow. Hence I'd like to ask you to come Monday rather than tomorrow—unless some errand brings you into the neighborhood, in which case you could also come tomorrow at your own risk. I am very much yearning for you, last flower of my lugubrious autumn, gracious fool. Tenderly madly, your devoted H.H. *P.S.: My brother is talking me to death. I am suffering very much. Please come soon!"*

•

At the beginning of December Heine was in such bad shape that, as he wrote to his French publisher, a number of Germans who had come to see the World's Fair delayed their return in the hope of also being able to attend his funeral. The fact that James de Rothschild had not only responded favorably to his request but, on his own initiative, had quietly registered shares of several new issues in Heine's name since then encouraged him to try his luck also with Baron Anselm, head of the Austrian branch of the Rothschild empire, with a less than subtle appeal for solidarity in "the two-thousand-year-old struggle against the common enemy." In his immediate and gracious reply Anselm, making the handout appear like a regular commercial transaction, in effect made him a present of a hundred shares, in line with an as yet largely personal, subjective brand of philanthropy which combined the ethics of ancestral tradition with a sense of *noblesse oblige* and guided the Rothschilds' pioneering efforts in this field.

For the New Year Heine sent the Mouche a box of chocolates, with a kind of apology:

I know very well that you don't like my observing conventions of this sort, but I am also doing it because of our external surroundings, who would interpret my non-observing the customary formalities as a lack of mutual esteem. I love you so much that, as far as I am concerned, I wouldn't even have to esteem you. You are my darling Mouche, and I feel my pains less whenever I think of your delicacy, the grace of your spirit. Unfortunately I can do no more for you than offer you such words, "coined air." My best wishes for the New Year—I won't say them. Words, words. Tomorrow I may perhaps be in good enough shape to see my Mouche, in which case I'll let her know. But in any case, on the day after tomorrow she'll see her Nebuchadnezzar II, former royal Prussian atheist, now worshipper of the lotus flower.

But his strength was rapidly giving out. The following day he informed her that after coughing for twenty-four hours straight he had come down with a terrible headache and could not see her until at least Friday. "I am almost going out of my mind with anger, pain, and impatience. I am going to complain to the Animal Protection League about a God who tortures me so cruelly."

On January 22, 1856, he again canceled one of her visits, writing in English: "*My brain is full of madness and my heart is full of sorrow.* Never was a poet more miserable amidst a happiness that seems to mock me. *Je pose une empreinte vivante* on all your treasures—but only in my thoughts. That is all you can have from me, *poor girl.*" The following day he complained about his right eye also giving him trouble and making it almost impossible for him to write. "But I love you very much and think of you a great deal, my sweetest. Your novella did not bore me in the least and gives me good hope for the future. You are not as stupid as you look. Graceful you are beyond measure, and it gladdens my senses . . . I am in a weepy mood. My heart yawns spasmodically. These yawns are unbearable. I wish I were dead or else a healthy fellow who no longer needs enemas."

·

She was not only "not as stupid as she looked," she was also probably neither as young nor as innocent as he may have believed, but within the confines of his room, his mind, and his heart, she was whatever he needed her to be. She brought light into the almost unrelieved darkness, she offered him the taste of life remembered, she unfroze time for him once again and gave him something to look forward to other than page proofs, opium, and death:

> *Lass mich mit glühenden Zangen kneipen,*
> *Lass grausam schinden mein Gesicht,*
> *Lass mich mit Ruten peitschen, stäupen—*
> *Nur warten, warten lass mich nicht!*
>
> *(Let pincers nip my flesh red-hot,*
> *Let me be flayed from sole to pate,*
> *Or whipped with scourges—but do not*
> *Make me just wait and wait and wait!)*

In five of the six poems inspired by the Mouche, the last ones he ever wrote, Heine achieved a limpid, almost playful simplicity of language that raises his characteristic blend of irony and resignation to the level of near-wisdom, or at the very least, the kind of defiance in the face of death that transcends mere courage:

> *Wahrhaftig, wir beide bilden*
> *Ein kurioses Paar,*
> *Die Liebste ist schwach auf den Beinen,*
> *Der Liebhaber lahm sogar.*
>
> *Sie ist ein leidendes Kätzchen,*
> *Und er ist krank wie ein Hund,*
> *Ich glaube, im Kopfe sind beide*
> *Nicht sonderlich gesund.*
>
> *(Truly the two of us make for*
> *A rather curious pair*
> *The beloved is weak on her legs, and*
> *The lover even limps.*
>
> *She is an ailing pussycat*
> *And he is sick as a dog,*
> *In their heads, I think, they neither*
> *Are altogether right.)*

It is not entirely clear whether, as Meissner claimed, the sixth and longest poem—148 lines—really was Heine's last, written three weeks before his death. (It was also Meissner who gave it the title "Für die Mouche," under which it has become generally known.) Internal evidence, including Heine's fast-deteriorating physical condition, suggests that it may actually have been written in November 1855, but the date hardly matters; it is in a very real sense a final summing up of his theme in language never more forceful or authoritative—the struggle between Nazarene and Hellene, eternal and irreconcilable beyond any poetic synthesis. With the poet lying in an ornate sarcophagus decorated with elaborate carvings from both his classical and his biblical traditions, he dreams of a passionflower turning into the mute, inaccessible beloved, their silent dialogue cut short by the carvings come to life and once again girding for battle:

> O, dieser Streit wird enden nimmermehr,
> Stets wird die Wahrheit hadern mit dem Schönen,
> Stets wird geschieden sein der Menschheit Heer
> In zwei Partei'n: Barbaren und Hellenen.

> (This strife can never end or yet remit;
> Truth always fights with Beauty in these scenes.
> The hosts of mankind always will be split
> Into two camps: Barbarians and Hellenes.)

"Für die Mouche" was Heine's farewell to love and the world. An exit worthy of him in every way.

CONSIDERING HEINE'S record of improbable survival against the odds, Dr. Gruby could scarcely be blamed for believing that his patient would go on living for another year or two, if not forever. But by the end of 1855 Heine's condition had deteriorated to an alarming degree, and with the new year came almost complete collapse, although he still continued to put in several hours of work every day whenever his crippling migraine headaches subsided temporarily.

Camille Selden saw Heine for the last time on Wednesday, February 13. She had herself been ill, he seemed even weaker than usual, and their meeting left her understandably depressed. She was supposed to return the following day, but he sent her what apparently were the last lines he ever wrote: "Darling, don't come today [Thursday], I have the most horrible migraine. Come tomorrow [Friday]. Your long-suffering H.H." On Friday she was herself under the weather and canceled the appointment, and by Saturday Heine's condition was such that she could no longer be admitted. Dr. Gruby prescribed a number of medications, but toward evening Heine simply refused to take anything further. The nurse, Catherine Bourlois, in her letter of March 11 reported to Heine's sister, Charlotte, that the day before his death he told her how happy he was to have seen his family, "because I am not going to see them anymore," and that he was sorry not to have written on Wednesday, when he was still able to do so.

On the last night [she went on] he kept repeating, "I am lost." During that fatal night I had a helper with me, and I went to wake up Miss Pauline when I saw the end approaching. I would have called Madame, but the slightest noise could have worsened his last moments, and I was afraid of the effect that her husband's death could have on her. However, at the supreme moment Miss Pauline ran to wake Madame, but all I could say to her as she appeared was that everything was over. A quarter of an hour prior to his death Herr Heine was still fully conscious. I constantly encouraged and comforted him to the best of my ability, but he realized that the medications no longer brought any relief. Because of his love for you, as well as the request you made before leaving here, I felt it my duty to write to you. But I have done so without informing Frau Heine, and I would appreciate your not mentioning my letters to her . . . I might add that on Saturday, between 4 and 5 p.m., Herr Heine called me three times and told me to write—but I did not understand what he was saying, and because I did not want him to keep talking, I said yes. Shortly thereafter I told him: When you stop throwing up, you'll write yourself, to which he replied: I am dying.

Thus Heine's authentic last words were apparently lost to the world, but chances are that they were much less quotable than his famous though probably apocryphal reply to a well-meaning friend who urged him on his deathbed to make his peace with the Lord: *"Dieu me pardonnera. C'est son métier."*

He died at 5 a.m. the following morning, February 17, 1856, aged fifty-eight years and two months.

•

The funeral took place on February 20, a chilly Wednesday morning. As the mourners assembled in the apartment, they discovered to their consternation that the widow had disappeared an hour and a half earlier. Mathilde not only did not accompany her husband's remains but in fact did not turn up again until several months later. In a letter to

Engels commenting on Heine's death, Marx cited what seemed to him some rather prescient lines by the poet:

> Um Sechse des Morgens war er gehenkt,
> Um Sieben ward er ins Grab gesenkt;
> Sie aber schon um achte
> Trank roten Wein und lachte.

> (At six in the morning he was hanged
> At seven lowered into the grave;
> She, however, by eight o'clock
> Already drank red wine and laughed.)

"He had foreseen exactly what came to pass," Marx wrote. "His body still lay in the house when, on the day of the funeral, the sweet angelic Mathilde waited at the door for the *maquereau* who was going to pick her up." Marx had always hated her, and he knew very little about people, including himself. Which does not necessarily invalidate his cynical view of the enigmatic Mathilde and her rather inexplicable behavior.

The simple ceremony at the Montmartre cemetery was attended by about a hundred people, among them Alexandre Dumas *père*, Théophile Gautier, the historian François Mignet, and Camille Selden. The plain tombstone was in later years replaced by a bust.

•

He would, one suspects, have been pleased to know that in death as in life he continued to be a figure of controversy.

Shortly after Heine's death, Campe sought his as yet unpublished poems for the Collected Edition, but whatever the vagaries of justice human or divine, poetic justice does seem on occasion to prevail. Had it not been for his stubborn stinginess and greed, he could no doubt have obtained the rights from Heine himself for relatively little money; now, instead of dealing with a poet whom he had—not inaccurately—characterized as stupid in matters of business, he had to contend with the poet's widow. Having re-emerged from wherever it was she spent the couple of months after her disappearance—the faithful Pauline in the meantime acting as intermediary with the outside world without betraying her secret—Mathilde teamed up with Henri Julia, a journalist and businessman with whom Heine had been on friendly terms since 1832 and whom he had appointed his testamentary executor. In the same Last Will and Testament of 1851, however, he had also stipulated that all his papers be turned over to Charlotte's son, Ludwig van Emden, but Mathilde and Julia simply chose to ignore that clause. Instead, determined to exact as high a price as possible for the rather formidable mass of unpublished manuscripts, they attempted some sort of triage, but with neither of them having any German, they could only separate the prose from what looked like poetry and finally commissioned Meissner in 1856 to put together a volume of the lyrics for Campe. Mathilde, however, refused to part with the originals. Campe in turn refused to accept copies—even the originals, as he correctly pointed out, were barely legible—and Meissner, just to further muddy the waters, omitted the poems to the Mouche, presumably for personal reasons, so that the first Collected Works of 1861 left out all the literary remains. Driven exclusively by greed, Mathilde and Julia sold off odds and ends and even tried to interest both the Prussian and the Austrian governments in preemptively acquiring the Heine papers so as to prevent their eventual publication. The two of them finally quarreled over money, as such friends are apt to, and in 1869 Mathilde sold everything but the *Memoirs* to Campe for 10,000 francs. After her death in 1883, Julia finally sold them to Campe, who published them together with a number of poems in the second supplementary volume to the Collected Works.

•

In the German Imperial Reich, united under Prussian tutelage by Bismarck in 1871 after the defeat of the French, Heine was widely regarded as subversive, Francophile, and above all a Jew, three not inaccurate if somewhat oversimplified characterizations, each of which the Teutomaniacal squareheads increasingly dominant in the new country's cultural and literary establishments construed as a capital crime. A prime example was the highly influential historian Heinrich von Treitschke, for whom Heine was a sworn enemy of Prussia in the pay of France: "With Börne and Heine began the irruption of the Jews into our literary history, an ugly and infertile interlude which fortunately did not last long." In fact, it came to a definite end in March of 1933, when Treitschke's theoretical strictures were translated into action by his brown-shirted spiritual descendant and all of Heine's writings were burned in public auto-dafés all over Germany. How many, among the millions watching those pyres on the town squares, recalled the prophetic line from Heine's "Almansor": " 'Twas but a prelude. For where books are burned, they end up burning people."

The man who provoked controversy all his life has remained an embattled figure in his native land ever since. No small achievement of itself, although all things considered, it ultimately says a great deal more about Germany than it does about Heine without lending itself to sweeping generalizations about either. There was Treitschke, to be sure, representing the increasingly virulent strain of racist nationalism that ended in the ultimate *Götterdämmerung*. But Heine's books continued to sell, and dissenting voices

[*192*]

persisted, at least until silenced by Nazi terror. Nietzsche called him the greatest lyricist in the German language—"He possessed that divine malice without which I cannot conceive of perfection." Nor did the Final Solution prove all that final for Heine; the troubles he caused in post-Nazi Germany, some of them verging on the grotesque, demonstrate that unlike the certifiably Teutonic *Dichter und Denker* of classical stature long since transformed into pigeon roosts, he still retains the power to start riots, even in effigy. Attempts to erect Heine monuments in several at the time West German cities led to protest demonstrations and local government crises, and a proposal in 1953 to rename the University of Düsseldorf, his hometown, after him was soundly defeated after a long and acrimonious debate. In what used to be East Germany, on the other hand, he was used as a totemic figure to legitimize the Communist regime, a revolutionary exiled along with Marx and Engels as a resolute opponent of the bourgeoisie.

This process of more or less simplistic politicization has tended to distort the core identity of the man, the more so since his poetic reputation in Germany underwent an inevitable eclipse with the rise of the modernist movement around the First World War. For the likes of Stefan George, Rilke, Hofmannsthal, the romantic, popular, overanthologized and set-to-music Heine of the *Book of Songs* was neither a model nor a worthy ancestor. Nor, for that matter, would Heine in turn have been likely to claim them as his spiritual descendants. Partly perhaps as a result, the poetry of his later years, and in particular the work he wrested from his seven-year agony, never received the attention it deserved, at least not in Germany. The French, on the other hand, responded to Heine with unstinting enthusiasm from the very outset and were quick to discern the radical departure marked by the late poems. Aided by some first-rate translations and by his own active participation in the arrangements for publication, he was almost as widely read in France as in Germany and was certainly appreciated with considerably less ambivalence. When, after World War II, the important Schocken collection of Heine material came on the market, de Gaulle personally issued orders to top any outside bids so as to make sure that it would remain in France; it is now deposited in the Bibliothèque Nationale.

.

Many of even his warmest admirers have felt obliged to pass moral judgment on Heine and found him wanting. He was often petty, vindictive, given to slander, self-pity, and self-aggrandizement, inconsistent in his opinions and unwilling to commit himself. That he could also be kind and generous and treated his wife with uncommon affection hardly counted in the balance.

There is some truth to almost everything that can be said about him, and this complexity may well hold the clue to his enduring power to disturb. But ultimately he defined himself quite clearly in the two crucial areas of his life.

He was a poet. His image of himself as a *German* poet was an illusion understandable enough at a time when Jews began to believe that they could be Germans. He wrote a German few Germans could match, and he drew his inspiration—whether he knew it or not—from the skepticism of generations of his ancestors, thus becoming the emblematic figure of an emancipation that went wrong from the very beginning—the outsider who is neither Jew nor German.

And he dealt with his dying in a way that far transcended mere courage and gave it a meaning few men have been able to wrest from it. Let those quick to condemn his all too human weaknesses match the grandeur of that end.

# A Selection of

# Heinrich Heine's Poems

# in German and English

*The English translations are drawn from*
The Complete Poems of Heinrich Heine:
A Modern English Version by Hal Draper
*published by Suhrkamp/Insel in 1982.*

## Lamentationen

Das Glück ist eine leichte Dirne,
Und weilt nicht gern am selben Ort;
Sie streicht das Haar dir von der Stirne
Und küßt dich rasch und flattert fort.

Frau Unglück hat im Gegenteile
Dich liebefest ans Herz gedrückt;
Sie sagt, sie habe keine Eile,
Setzt sich zu dir ans Bett und strickt.

## *Lamentations*

Happiness is a giddy girl
And always disinclined to stay;
She pats your head, gives you a whirl,
Kisses you quick, and flits away.

But Lady Sorrow now! Don't worry,
She's just the very opposite:
She holds you fast—she's in no hurry—
She sits down by your bed to knit.

## Jetzt Wohin?

Jetzt wohin? Der dumme Fuß
Will mich gern nach Deutschland tragen;
Doch es schüttelt klug das Haupt
Mein Verstand und scheint zu sagen:

«Zwar beendigt ist der Krieg,
Doch die Kriegsgerichte blieben,
Und es heißt, du habest einst
Viel Erschießliches geschrieben.»

Das ist wahr, unangenehm
Wär mir das Erschossenwerden;
Bin kein Held, es fehlen mir
Die pathetischen Gebärden.

Gern würd ich nach England gehn,
Wären dort nicht Kohlendämpfe
Und Engländer—schon ihr Duft
Gibt Erbrechen mir und Krämpfe.

Manchmal kommt mir in den Sinn,
Nach Amerika zu segeln,
Nach dem großen Freiheitstall,
Der bewohnt von Gleichheitsflegeln—

Doch es ängstet mich ein Land,
Wo die Menschen Tabak käuen,
Wo sie ohne König kegeln,
Wo sie ohne Spucknapf speien.

## *Now, Where To?*

Now, where to? My foolish feet
Want to go to Germany;
But my reason shakes its head
Wisely, and it says to me:

"True, the war is ended now,
But the wartime laws are not,
And it's said that you once wrote
Stuff enough to get you shot."

Yes, this shooting isn't nice;
I'm no hero, as is known,
And no good at gestures made
To be suitably high flown.

I would go to England but
There is all that coalmino damp
And those English—*ach*, their smell
Gives me nausea and cramp.

I have sometimes thought to sail
To America the Free,
To that Freedom Stable where
All the boors live equally.

But I fear a land where men
Chew tobacco in platoons,
There's no king among the pins,
And they spit without spittoons.

Rußland, dieses schöne Reich,
Würde mir vielleicht behagen,
Doch im Winter könnte ich
Dort die Knute nicht ertragen.

Traurig schau ich in die Höh',
Wo viel tausend Sterne nicken—
Aber meinen eignen Stern
Kann ich nirgens dort erblicken.

Hat im güldnen Labyrinth
Sich vielleicht verirrt am Himmel,
Wie ich selber mich verirrt
In dem irdischen Getümmel.—

Russia? It might be a fine
Place in which to gad about,
But in winter I'm not sure
I could learn to bear the knout.

Sadly gazing to the sky
I see stars in thousands there—
But the star that is my own,
I can't see it anywhere.

Maybe it has lost its way
In a maze that's silver-pearled,
Just as I myself am lost
In the tumult of the world.

## Unvollkommenheit

Nichts ist vollkommen hier auf dieser Welt.
Der Rose ist der Stachel beigesellt;
Ich glaube gar, die lieben holden Engel
Im Himmel droben sind nicht ohne Mängel.

Der Tulpe fehlt der Duft. Es heißt am Rhein:
Auch Ehrlich stahl einmal ein Ferkelschwein.
Hätte Lucretia sich nicht erstochen,
Sie wär vielleicht gekommen in die Wochen.

Häßliche Füße hat der stolze Pfau.
Uns kann die amüsant geistreichste Frau
Manchmal langweilen wie die Henriade
Voltaires, sogar wie Klopstocks Messiade.

Die bravste, klügste Kuh kein Spanisch weiß,
Wie Maßmann kein Latein—Der Marmorsteiß
Der Venus von Canova ist zu glatte,
Wie Maßmanns Nase viel zu ärschig platte.

Im süßen Lied ist oft ein saurer Reim,
Wie Bienenstachel steckt im Honigseim.
Am Fuß verwundbar war der Sohn der Thetis,
Und Alexander Dumas ist ein Metis.

Der strahlenreinste Stern am Himmelzelt,
Wenn er den Schnupfen kriegt, herunterfällt.
Der beste Äpfelwein schmeckt nach der Tonne,
Und schwarze Flecken sieht man in der Sonne.

## *Imperfection*

Nothing is perfect in this world below.
There is no rose without the thorn also.
In Heaven too: I sometimes wonder whether
The angels have no failings altogether.

The tulip has no scent. Rhinelanders say:
Even His Honor stole a pig one day.
Lucretia stabbed herself when overmastered—
Who knows but what she would have borne a bastard?

The peacock that's so proud has ugly feet.
A woman may be witty, gifted, sweet,
Yet often bore us, like the Henriade
Of Voltaire or like Klopstock's Messiade.

The finest cow, like Massmann, has no mind
For Latin; and the marbleized behind
Of Canova's Venus is too sleek and dumpy,
While Massmann's nose is far too flat and rumpy.

The sweetest song may have its sour rhymes,
And bee stings lurk in honey oftentimes.
Achilles had his heel—recall the motto—
And Alexander Dumas's a mulatto.

The brightest, purest star the heavens hold
Will fall to earth if once it catches cold.
The barrel taste of cider's an objection,
And spots are seen upon the sun's complexion.

Du bist, verehrte Frau, du selbst sogar
Nicht fehlerfrei, nicht aller Mängel bar.
Du schaust mich an—du fragst mich, was dir fehle?
Ein Busen, und im Busen eine Seele.

You too, my honored lady, are not free
From blemishes and faults entirely.
What do you lack? You want to know this minute:
A bosom, and a heart that beats within it.

## Gedächtnisfeier

Keine Messe wird man singen,
Keinen Kadosch wird man sagen,
Nichts gesagt und nichts gesungen
Wird an meinen Sterbetagen.

Doch vielleicht an solchem Tage,
Wenn das Wetter schön und milde,
Geht spazieren auf Montmartre
Mit Paulinen Frau Mathilde.

Mit dem Kranz von Immortellen
Kommt sie, mir das Grab zu schmücken,
Und sie seufzet: «Pauvre homme!"
Feuchte Wehmut in den Blicken.

Leider wohn ich viel zu hoch,
Und ich habe meiner Süßen
Keinen Stuhl hier anzubieten;
Ach! sie schwankt mit müden Füßen.

Süßes, dickes Kind, du darfst
Nicht zu Fuß nach Hause gehen;
An dem Barrieregitter
Siehst du die Fiaker stehen.

## Commemoration Service

Not a mass will be sung for me,
Not a *Kaddish* will be said,
None will say or sing a service
On the day that I lie dead.

But on some such day it may be,
If good weather is foreseen,
Ma'm Mathilde will go strolling
On Montmartre with Pauline.

She will come to deck my grave with
Immortelles, and say with sighs:
*"Pauvre homme!"* and wipe a teardrop
Of damp sorrow from her eyes.

But, alas, I shall be living
Too high up—there'll be no seat
I can offer to my darling
As she sways on weary feet.

Oh you sweet and chubby child, you
Must not walk home all the way;
You'll see coaches standing ready
At the barrier gate that day.

# Im Oktober 1849

Gelegt hat sich der starke Wind,
Und wieder stille wird's daheime;
Germania, das große Kind,
Erfreut sich wieder seiner Weihnachtsbäume.

Wir treiben jetzt Familienglück—
Was höher lockt, das ist vom Übel—
Die Friedensschwalbe kehrt zurück,
Die einst genistet in des Hauses Giebel.

Gemütlich ruhen Wald und Fluß,
Von sanftem Mondlicht übergossen;
Nur manchmal knallt's—Ist das ein Schuß?—
Es ist vielleicht ein Freund, den man erschossen.

Vielleicht mit Waffen in der Hand
Hat man den Tollkopf angetroffen
(Nicht jeder hat soviel Verstand
Wie Flaccus, der so kühn davongeloffen).

Es knallt. Es ist ein Fest vielleicht,
Ein Feuerwerk zur Goethefeier!—
Die Sontag, die dem Grab entsteigt,
Begrüßt Raketenlärm—die alte Leier.

Ausch Liszt taucht wieder auf, der Franz,
Er lebt, er liegt nicht blutgerötet
Auf einem Schlachtfeld Ungarlands;
Kein Russe noch Kroat' hat ihn getötet.

## *In October 1849*

The tempest's gone, the wind is mild,
At home it's fallen still once more;
Germania, that great big child,
Enjoys his Christmas tree just as before.

For family happiness we yearn—
A higher aim's an evil thing—
In peace the swallows now return,
Again they nest on gable roofs and sing.

In woods the quiet rillets run,
Soft moonlight bathes the garden plot,
But sometimes *bang*—Was that a gun?—
Perhaps it is a friend who has been shot.

Perhaps they caught him, arms in hand,
That firebrand who would not obey—
(Not everyone can understand
Like Horace when it's brave to run away.)

A *bang:* perhaps the rockets boom
For Goethe's anniversary,
Or Sontag raised up from the tomb,
Old lyre in hand, by such a noisy spree.

And Liszt shows up again, revealed
As still alive, not gory-red
On some Hungarian battlefield;
No Russian or Croatian struck him dead.

Es fiel der Freiheit letzte Schanz',
Und Ungarn blutet sich zu Tode—
Doch unversehrt blieb Ritter Franz,
Sein Säbel auch—er liegt in der Kommode.

Er lebt, der Franz, und wird als Greis
Vom Ungarkriege Wunderdinge
Erzählen in der Enkel Kreis—
«So lag ich und so führt ich meine Klinge!"

Wenn ich den Namen Ungarn hör,
Wird mir das deutsche Wams zu enge,
Es braust darunter wie ein Meer,
Mit ist, als grüßten mich Trompetenklänge!

Es klirrt mir wieder im Gemüt
Die Heldensage, längst verklungen,
Das eisern wilde Kämpenlied—
Das Lied vom Untergang der Nibelungen.

Es ist dasselbe Heldenlos,
Es sind dieselben alten Mären,
Die Namen sind verändert bloß,
Doch sind's dieselben «Helden lobebären."

Es ist dasselbe Schicksal auch—
Wie stolz und frei die Fahnen fliegen,
Es muß der Held, nach altem Brauch,
Den tierisch rohen Mächten unterliegen.

Und diesmal hat der Ochse gar
Mit Bären einen Bund geschlossen—
Du fällst; doch tröste dich, Magyar,
Wir andre haben schlimmre Schmach genossen.

Freedom's last trench was overmatched,
And Hungary is at death's door—
But Franz, brave knight, emerged unscratched,
His saber too—it's lying in his drawer.

Franz lives; and when his hair is gray,
Amidst his grandsons—to anoint
The tale with wonders—he will say:
" 'Twas here I lay, and thus I bore my point."

When I hear Hungary's name outcried,
My German jacket binds too tight,
I feel a roaring sea inside,
I hear the call of trumpets in the night!

Again within my soul I hear
Old sagas they no longer tell,
Wild battle songs of sword and spear—
The song of how the Nibelungen fell.

The lot of heroes is the same,
The same old story anyhow,
They simply change around the name,
But it's the same "praiseworthy heroes" now.

They also have the same old fate:
Though banners proudly wave, of course,
The hero must, as customs state,
Be overthrown by raw and brutish force.

This time, indeed, the ox and bear
Have made alliance, on all fours:
You fall; but, Magyars, don't despair,
For we endure a shame that's worse than yours.

Anständ'ge Bestien sind es doch,
Die ganz honett dich überwunden;
Doch wir geraten in das Joch
Von Wölfen, Schweinen und gemeinen Hunden.

Das heult und bellt und grunzt—ich kann
Ertragen kaum den Duft der Sieger.
Doch still, Poet, das greift dich an—
Du bist so krank, und schweigen wäre klüger.

They're decent beasts, at least, who broke
Your forces honestly, in fine;
But we are bent beneath the yoke
Of wolves and common curs and filthy swine.

They howl and bark—I can't abide
The victor's stench that taints the skies.
But poet, hush—it hurts inside—
You are so sick and silence would be wise.

## Ruhelechzend

Laß bluten deine Wunden, laß
Die Tränen fließen unaufhaltsam—
Geheime Wollust schwelgt im Schmerz,
Und Weinen ist ein süßer Balsam.

Verwundet dich nicht fremde Hand,
So mußt du selber dich verletzen;
Auch danke hübsch dem lieben Gott,
Wenn Zähren deine Wangen netzen.

Des Tages Lärm verhallt, es steigt
Die Nacht herab mit langen Flören.
In ihrem Schoße wird kein Schelm,
Kein Tölpel deine Ruhe stören.

Hier bist du sicher vor Musik,
Vor des Pianofortes Folter,
Und vor der großen Oper Pracht
Und schrecklichem Bravourgepolter.

Hier wirst du nicht verfolgt, geplagt
Vom eitlen Virtuosenpacke
Und vom Genie Giacomos
Und seiner Weltberühmtheitsclaque.

O Grab, du bist das Paradies
Für pöbelscheue, zarte Ohren—
Der Tod ist gut, doch besser wär's,
Die Mutter hätt uns nie geboren.

## Longing for Rest

Oh, let your wounds bleed on unchecked,
And let your tears flow wild or calm—
In pain there burns a secret joy,
And weeping is a kindly balm.

Had others' hands not wounded you,
Yourself would have to deal the hurt;
So give your gracious thanks to God
When down your cheeks the teardrops spurt.

The noise of day is hushed; the night
Falls veiled with crape upon her breast;
And in her lap no knave or fool
Will come by to disturb your rest.

You're safe from music's bluster there,
From torment by pianos clanging,
From operatic tinsel pomp
And din of dread bravura banging.

You won't be dogged or plagued there by
The peacock virtuoso pack,
By Giacomo's great genius and
His worldwide advertising claque.

O grave, you're paradise for ears
That shun the rabble's brawl with scorn—
Death's good, but it were better still
If we had never yet been born.

## Im Mai

Die Freunde, die ich geküßt und geliebt,
Die haben das Schlimmste an mir verübt.
Mein Herze bricht; doch droben die Sonne,
Lachend begrüßt sie den Monat der Wonne.

Es blüht der Lenz. Im grünen Wald
Der lustige Vogelgesang erschallt,
Und Mädchen und Blumen, sie lächeln jungfräulich—
O schöne Welt, du bist abscheulich!

Da lob ich mir den Orkus fast;
Dort kränkt uns nirgends ein schnöder Kontrast;
Für leidende Herzen ist es viel besser
Dort unten am stygischen Nachtgewässer.

Sein melancholisches Geräusch,
Der Stymphaliden ödes Gekreisch,
Der Furien Singsang, so schrill und grell,
Dazwischen des Zerberus Gebell—

Das paßt verdrießlich zu Unglück und Qual—
Im Schattenreich, dem traurigen Tal,
In Proserpinens verdammten Domänen,
Ist alles im Einklang mit unseren Tränen.

Hier oben aber, wie grausamlich
Sonne und Rosen stechen sie mich!
Mich höhnt der Himmel, der bläulich und mailich—
O schöne Welt, du bist abscheulich!

## *In May*

The friends I kissed and loved I recall
Were those that treated me worst of all.
My heart is breaking; but bright and gay
The sun laughs greetings down on May.

The sweet spring blooms. The greenwoods ring
With merry birdsong echoing,
Flowers and girls wear a virginal smile—
O beautiful world, you're hideously vile!

I'd almost praise Orcus in despair:
No cruel contrast wounds us there;
For suffering hearts it's better below
Where Styx's night-black waters flow.

Its melancholy plashing wave,
Stymphalides that shriek and rave,
The way the Furies shrill and squall,
Cerberus baying through it all—

All this suits woe and pain so well—
In that sad vale where shadows dwell,
In Proserpine's accursèd spheres
All harmonizes with our tears.

But here above, how cruelly
Sunlight and roses stab at me!
May's blue sky mocks me with a smile—
O beautiful world, you're hideously vile!

## Babylonische Sorgen

Mich ruft der Tod—Ich wollt', o Süße,
Daß ich dich in einem Wald verließe,
In einem jener Tannenforsten,
Wo Wölfe heulen, Geier horsten
Und schrecklich grunzt die wilde Sau,
Des blonden Ebers Ehefrau.

Mich ruft der Tod—Es wär noch besser,
Müßt ich auf hohem Seegewässer
Verlasen dich, mein Weib, mein Kind,
Wenngleich der tolle Nordpolwind
Dort peitscht die Wellen, und aus den Tiefen
Die Ungetüme, die dort schliefen,
Haifisch' und Krokodile, kommen
Mit offnem Rachen emporgeschwommen—
Glaub mir, mein Kind, mein Weib, Mathilde,
Nicht so gefährlich ist das wilde,
Erzürnte Meer und der trotzige Wald
Als unser jetziger Aufenthalt!
Wie schrecklich auch der Wolf und der Geier,
Haifische und sonstige Meerungeheuer:
Viel grimmere, schlimmere Bestien enthält
Paris, die leuchtende Hauptstadt der Welt,
Das singende, springende, schöne Paris,
Die Hölle der Engel, der Teufel Paradies—
Daß ich dich hier verlassen soll,
Das macht mich verrückt, das macht mich toll!

Mit spöttischem Sumsen mein Bett umschwirrn
Die schwarzen Fliegen; auf Nas' und Stirn

## Babylonian Anxieties

Death calls me. I'd prefer, my own,
To leave you in a wood alone,
In one of those fir forests where
The vultures nest, wolves make their lair,
And savage sows grunt low and wait,
The blond-haired boar's still wilder mate.

Death calls me. Better still would be
If I could leave you on the sea,
The lonely sea, my woman-child,
Though fierce north winds were raging wild
And lashed the waves, while from the deep
Grim monsters, wakened from their sleep,
The sharks and crocodiles, came by
With gaping jaw and glaring eye—
Believe me, Mathilde, woman-child,
Less danger lies out in the wild
Expanse of sea or woods of fear
Than in the place we sojourn here!
Fearsome though wolves and vultures be,
Or sharks and monsters of the sea,
Far fiercer beasts prowl through the night
In this world capital of light,
Paris, the lilting, lovely belle—
The devils' Eden, the angels' Hell.
To think it's here I leave you behind—
It drives me mad, it rocks my mind!

Mockingly buzzing round my bed,
Black flies settle on my head

Setzen sie sich—fatales Gelichter!
Etwelche haben wie Menschengesichter,
Auch Elefantenrüssel daran,
Wie Gott Ganesa in Hindostan.——
In meinem Hirne rumort es und knackt,
Ich glaube, da wird ein Koffer gepackt,
Und mein Verstand reist ab—o wehe!—
Noch früher, als ich selber gehe.

And on my nose—a nasty crew!
Some have human faces too,
Plus elephant trunks on the face of a man
Like the god Ganesa in Hindustan.—
With bedlam and banging my brain is wracked:
I think a trunk is being packed—
My reason will depart—ah woe!—
Ere I myself am set to go.

# Das Sklavenschiff

Der Superkargo Mynheer van Koek
Sitzt rechnend in seiner Kajüte;
Er kalkuliert der Ladung Betrag
Und die probabeln Profite.

«Der Gummi ist gut, der Pfeffer ist gut,
Dreihundert Säcke und Fässer;
Ich habe Goldstaub und Elfenbein—
Die schwarze Ware ist besser.

Sechshundert Neger tauschte ich ein
Spottwohlfeil am Senegalflusse.
Das Fleisch ist hart, die Sehnen sind stramm,
Wie Eisen vom besten Gusse.

Ich hab zum Tausche Branntewein,
Glasperlen und Stahlzeug gegeben;
Gewinne daran achthundert Prozent,
Bleibt mir die Hälfte am Leben.

Bleiben mir Neger dreihundert nur
Im Hafen von Rio-Janeiro,
Zahlt dort mir hundert Dukaten per Stück
Das Haus Gonzales Perreiro.»

Da plötzlich wird Mynheer van Koek
Aus seinen Gedanken gerissen;

## *The Slave Ship*

I

The supercargo Mynheer van Koek
Sits in his cabin, stocktaking;
He's reckoning up the shipment's size
And the probable profit he's making.

"The rubber is good, the pepper is good—
Three hundred barrels and sacks;
There's gold dust too, and ivory tusks—
But the best goods are the blacks.

"At Senegal River I got dirt-cheap
Six hundred Negroes in trade;
Their flesh is firm, their sinews strong,
Of iron are they made.

"I got them in trade for beads of glass,
Some brandy, and iron gear;
If only the half of them live, I'll make
Eight hundred percent all clear.

"If I still have only three hundred blacks
When we get to Rio d' Janeiro,
I'll get a hundred ducats a head
From the firm of Gonzales Perreiro."

Then suddenly Mynheer van Koek
Was interrupted. In came

Der Schiffschirurgius tritt herein,
Der Doktor van der Smissen.

Das ist eine klapperdürre Figur,
Die Nase voll roter Warzen—
»Nun, Wasserfeldscherer,« ruft van Koek,
»Wie geht's meinen lieben Schwarzen?«

Der Doktor dankt der Nachfrage und spricht:
»Ich bin zu melden gekommen,
Daß heute nacht die Sterblichkeit
Bedeutend zugenommen.

Im Durchschnitt starben täglich zwei,
Doch heute starben sieben,
Vier Männer, drei Frauen—Ich hab den Verlust
Sogleich in die Kladde geschrieben.

Ich inspizierte die Leichen genau;
Denn diese Schelme stellen
Sich manchmal tot, damit man sie
Hinabwirft in die Wellen.

Ich nahm den Toten die Eisen ab;
Und wie ich gewöhnlich tue,
Ich ließ die Leichen werfen ins Meer
Des Morgens in der Fruhe.

Es schossen alsbald hervor aus der Flut
Haifische, ganze Heere,
Sie lieben so sehr das Negerfleisch;
Das sind meine Pensionäre.

Sie folgten unseres Schiffes Spur,
Seit wir verlassen die Küste;

The little ship's surgeon through the door,
Van der Smissen by name.

His figure's bony, thin and dry,
His nose with warts is flaring—
"How goes it, sawbones," cried van Koek,
"How are my dear blacks faring?"

The doctor acknowledged the question, and said:
"I came here to announce
Last night the rate of death increased
By considerable amounts.

"The daily average death was two,
But seven died today,
Four men, three women—I had the loss
Put in the log straightway.

"I had the corpses closely checked,
For these rogues are rascally
And sometimes pretend to be dead so that
They'll get thrown into the sea

"The chains were taken off the dead,
And as I usually do,
I had the bodies cast overboard.
Before the morning was through.

"At once a swarm of sharks shot up
From deep down in the waters;
They like this black meat very much—
I consider them my boarders.

"They've followed in our wake since then
As the coastline faded from sight;

Die Bestien wittern den Leichengeruch
Mit schnupperndem Flaßgelüste.

Es ist possierlich anzusehn,
Wie sie nach den Toten schnappen!
Die faßt den Kopf, die faßt das Bein,
Die andern schlucken die Lappen.

Ist alles verschlungen, dann tummeln sie sich
Vergnügt um des Schiffes Planken
Und glotzen mich an, als wollten sie
Sich für das Frühstück bedanken."

Doch seufzend fällt ihm in die Red'
Van Koek: «Wie kann ich lindern
Das Übel? wie kann ich die Progression
Der Sterblichkeit verhindern?"

Der Doktor erwidert: «Durch eigne Schuld
Sind viele Schwarze gestorben;
Ihr schlechter Odem hat die Luft
Im Schiffsraum so sehr verdorben.

Auch starben viele durch Melancholie,
Dieweil sie sich tödlich langweilen;
Durch etwas Luft, Musik und Tanz
Läßt sich die Krankheit heilen."

Da ruft van Koek: «Ein guter Rat!
Mein teurer Wasserfeldscherer
Ist klug wie Aristoteles,
Des Alexanders Lehrer.

Der Präsident der Sozietät
Der Tulpenveredlung im Delfte

The beasts snuff at the corpses' scent
With a gourmand's appetite.

"It's a comical sight to see them rush
In at the bodies and snap!
One gobbles a head, another a leg,
A third grabs a snippet or scrap.

"When all is devoured, they romp and frisk,
Sporting merrily at the ship's side,
And stare at me as if they would
Say thanks for the breakfast supplied."

But here with a sigh van Koek broke in:
"How can we ease this threat?
How can we stop this rate of death
From getting bigger yet?"

The doctor said: "It's their own fault
That so many blacks have died:
The bad breath in the hold has fouled
All of the air inside.

"For many it's melancholia
That simply bores them to death;
Some music and dancing will cure their ills,
Fresh air will mend their breath."

Then van Koek cried: "That's sound advice!
Dear sawbones, you sly creature,
You're smart as Aristotle, who
Was Alexander's teacher.

"The head of the Tulip Improvement League
In Delft is the clever kind

Ist sehr gescheit, doch hat er nicht
Von Eurem Verstande die Hälfte.

Musik! Musik! Die Schwarzen soll'n
Hier auf dem Verdecke tanzen.
Und wer sich beim Hopsen nicht amüsiert,
Den soll die Peitsche kuranzen."

## II

Hoch aus dem blauen Himmelszelt
Viel tausend Sterne schauen,
Sehnsüchtig glänzend, groß und klug,
Wie Augen von schönen Frauen.

Sie blicken hinunter in das Meer,
Das weithin überzogen
Mit phosphorstrahlendem Purpurduft;
Wollüstig girren die Wogen.

Kein Segel flattert am Sklavenschiff,
Es liegt wie abgetakelt;
Doch schimmern Laternen auf dem Verdeck,
Wo Tanzmusik spektakelt.

Die Fiedel streicht der Steuermann,
Der Koch, der spielt die Flöte,
Ein Schiffsjung' schlägt die Trommel dazu,
Der Doktor bläst die Trompete.

Wohl hundert Neger, Männer und Frauen,
Sie jauchzen und hopsen und kreisen
Wie toll herum; bei jedem Sprung
Taktmäßig klirren die Eisen.

But for thinking deep he doesn't have
A half of your powers of mind.

"Ho, music, music! The blacks shall have
A dance on the deck of the ship.
And whoever doesn't like to prance
Will get a taste of the whip."

II

High up on heaven's azure vault
A myriad stars arise,
Agleam with longing, knowing, bright
Like lovely women's eyes.

They look down on the glowing waves
Wrapped phosphorescently
In purple mist. Voluptuous
Murmurs rise from the sea.

The slave ship lies as if unrigged,
No sail is fluttering there;
But lanterns shimmer on the deck,
Dance music cleaves the air.

There, on a fiddle the helmsman saws,
On a flute the cook is playing,
A cabin boy beats away on a drum,
The doctor's trumpet is braying.

A hundred Negroes, women and men,
With madly whirling feet
Are reveling; with every leap
Chains clank in time with the beat.

Sie stampfen den Boden mit tobender Lust,
Und manche schwarze Schöne
Umschlingt wollüstig den nackten Genoß—
Dazwischen ächzende Töne.

Der Büttel ist Maître des plaisirs,
Und hat mit Peitschenhieben
Die lässigen Tänzer stimuliert,
Zum Frohsinn angetrieben.

Und Dideldumdei und Schnedderedeng!
Der Lärm lockt aus den Tiefen
Die Ungetüme der Wasserwelt,
Die dort blödsinnig schliefen.

Schlaftrunken kommen geschwommen heran
Haifische, viele hundert;
Sie glotzen nach dem Schiff hinauf,
Sie sind verdutzt, verwundert.

Sie merken, daß die Frühstückstund'
Noch nicht gekommen, und gähnen,
Ausperrend den Rachen; die Kiefer sind
Bepflanzt mit Sägezähnen.

Und Dideldumdei und Schnedderedeng—
Es nehmen kein Ende die Tänze.
Die Haifische beißen vor Ungeduld
Sich selber in die Schwänze.

Ich glaube, sie lieben nicht die Musik,
Wie viele von ihrem Gelichter.
«Trau keiner Bestie, die nicht liebt
Musik!" sagt Albions großer Dichter.

They stamp the planks with roars of joy,
And many a black-skinned belle
Embraces a naked partner in lust—
And groans are heard as well.

The master of revels is the guard;
With whiplash swinging free,
He goads the weary dancers on
To heights of frenzied glee.

And diddledum*dee* and tantara*ra*!
The uproar lures from the deep
The monsters of the water world
Who sleep their brutish sleep.

Still sleepy-eyed, a shoal of sharks
Swim up along the side;
They stare up blankly at the ship,
Puzzled and mystified.

The sharks take note that breakfast time
Has not yet come; their jaws
Are gaping open as they yawn—
Their teeth are rows of saws.

And diddledum*dee* and tantara*ra*—
The dance goes on without fail.
Impatient for their meal the sharks
Are biting each other's tail.

They don't like music, I believe—
Like others in this regard.
Don't trust a beast that has no love
For music, says Albion's bard.

Und Schnedderedeng und Dideldumdei—
Die Tänze nehmen kein Ende.
Am Fockmast steht Mynheer van Koek
Und faltet betend die Hände:

«Um Christi willen verschone, o Herr,
Das Leben der schwarzen Sünder!
Erzürnten sie dich, so weißt du ja,
Sie sind so dumm wie die Rinder.

Verschone ihr Leben um Christi will'n,
Der für uns alle gestorben!
Denn bleiben mir nicht dreihundert Stück,
So ist mein Geschäft verdorben."

And diddledum*dee* and tantara*ra*—
They dance without stop or stay.
At the foremast stands Mynheer van Koek
And he folds his hands to pray:

"For Jesus' sake, O Lord, spare these
Black sinners' lives here below!
If they offended you, after all
They're just dumb cattle, you know.

"Oh, spare their lives for Jesus' sake
Who did not die in vain!
For if I don't keep three hundred head
My business is down the drain."

# Zum Lazarus

## I

Laß die heil'gen Parabolen,
Laß die frommen Hypothesen—
Suche die verdammten Fragen
Ohne Umschweif uns zu lösen.

Warum schleppt sich blutend, elend,
Unter Kreuzlast der Gerechte,
Während glücklich als ein Sieger
Trabt auf hohem Roß der Schlechte?

Woran liegt die Schuld? Ist etwa
Unser Herr nicht ganz allmächtig?
Oder treibt er selbst den Unfug?
Ach, das wäre niederträchtig.

Also fragen wir beständig,
Bis man uns mit einer Handvoll
Erde endlich stopft die Mäuler—
Aber ist das eine Antwort?

## II

Es hatte mein Haupt die schwarze Frau
Zärtlich ans Herz geschlossen;
Ach! meine Haare wurden grau,
Wo ihre Tränen geflossen.

## *Supplement to "Lazarus"*

### I

Drop those holy parables and
Pietist hypotheses.
Answer us these damning questions—
No evasions, if you please.

Why do just men stagger, bleeding,
Crushed beneath their cross's weight,
While the wicked ride the high horse,
Happy victors blest by fate?

Who's to blame? Is God not mighty,
Not with power panoplied?
Or is evil His own doing?
Ah, that would be vile indeed.

Thus we ask and keep on asking,
Till a handful of cold clay
Stops our mouths at last securely—
But pray tell, is that an answer?

### II

It was the dark woman who pressed my head
Against her heart one day.
Ah, where her poisoned tears were shed
My hair has turned to gray.

Sie küßte mich lahm, sie küßte mich krank,
Sie küßte mir blind die Augen;
Das Mark aus meinem Rückgrat trank
Ihr Mund mit wildem Saugen.

Mein Leib ist jetzt ein Leichnam, worin
Der Geist ist eingekerkert—
Manchmal wird ihm unwirsch zu Sinn,
Er tobt und rast und berserkert.

Ohnmächtige Flüche! Dein schlimmster Fluch
Wird keine Fliege töten.
Ertrage die Schickung, und versuch,
Gelinde zu flennen, zu beten.

### III

Wie langsam kriechet sie dahin,
Die Zeit, die schauderhafte Schnecke!
Ich aber, ganz bewegungslos
Blieb ich hier auf demselben Flecke.

In meine dunkel Zelle dringt
Kein Sonnenstrahl, kein Hoffnungsschimmer,
Ich weiß, nur mit der Kirchhofsgruft
Vertausch ich dies fatale Zimmer.

Vielleicht bin ich gestorben längst;
Es sind vielleicht nur Spukgestalten
Die Phantasien, die des Nachts
Im Hirn den bunten Umzug halten.

Es mögen wohl Gespenster sein,
Altheidnisch göttlichen Gelichters;

She kissed me sick, she kissed me lame
And blind in these eyes of mine;
She wildly drank, in passion's name,
The strength from out my spine.

My body's now a corpse, a cage
That holds my soul in chains—
It shakes the bars in berserk rage,
It roars and storms and strains.

Impotent curses! all too weak
To slay a fly in air.
Bear your fate—it's time to seek
Comfort in whining, in prayer.

### III

How slowly time, the dreadful snail,
Comes crawling with its sluggish pace!
But I, who cannot stir at all,
Am fixed here in the selfsame place.

No gleam of sun, no ray of hope
Pierces this dark cell through the gloom;
I know that only for the grave
Shall I exchange this direful room.

Perhaps I have been long since dead;
Perhaps it's but a ghostly train
Of phantasies that march at night
In motley pageant through my brain.

They may be ghosts indeed, a pack
Of pagan gods of old who come

Sie wählen gern zum Tummelplatz
Den Schädel eines toten Dichters.—

Die schaurig süßen Orgia,
Das nächtlich tolle Geistertreiben,
Sucht des Poeten Leichenhand
Manchmal am Morgen aufzuschreiben.

IV

Einst sah ich viele Blumen blühen
An meinem Weg; jedoch zu faul,
Mich pflückend nieder zu bemühen,
Ritt ich vorbei auf stolzem Gaul.

Jetzt, wo ich todessiech und elend,
Jetzt, wo geschaufelt schon die Gruft,
Oft im Gedächtnis höhnend, quälend,
Spukt der verschmähten Blumen Duft.

Besonders eine feuergelbe
Viole brennt mir stets im Hirn.
Wie reut es mich, daß ich dieselbe
Nicht einst genoß, die tolle Dirn'.

Mein Trost ist: Lethes Wasser haben
Noch jetzt verloren nicht die Macht,
Das dumme Menschenherz zu laben
Mit des Vergessens süßer Nacht.

V

Ich sah sie lachen, sah sie lächeln,
Ich sah sie ganz zugrunde gehn;

To make a playground for their sport
In a dead poet's cranium.

These dread, sweet orgies of the night,
Mad revels of a spectral play—
Often the poet's lifeless hand
Will try to write them down next day.

IV

I once saw many a flower blowing
Upon my way; in indolence
I scorned to pluck them in my going
And passed in proud indifference.

Now, when my grave is dug, they taunt me;
Now, when I'm sick to death in pain,
In mocking torment still they haunt me,
The fragrant flowers of my disdain.

Above all, one of yellow fire,
A violet, burning, ravishing—
Ah, how I rue with bitter desire
I never enjoyed the wild young thing.

This is my comfort: Lethe's art still
Has not lost all its ancient might
To heal the stupid human heart still
With sweet oblivion's endless night.

V

I saw them laughing, saw them crying,
I saw them ruined, saw them smile;

Ich hört ihr Weinen und ihr Röcheln,
Und habe ruhig zugesehn.

Leidtragend folgt ich ihren Särgen,
Und bis zum Kirchhof ging ich mit;
Hernach, ich will es nicht verbergen,
Speist ich zu Mittag mit App'tit.

Doch jetzt auf einmal mit Betrübnis
Denk ich der längstverstorbnen Schar;
Wie lodernd plötzliche Verliebnis
Stürmt's auf im Herzen wunderbar!

Besonders sind es Julchens Tränen,
Die im Gedächtnis rinnen mir;
Die Wehmut wird zu wildem Sehnen,
Und Tag und Nacht ruf ich nach ihr!——

Oft kommt zu mir die tote Blume
Im Fiebertraum; alsdann zumut'
Ist mir, als böte sie postume
Gewährung meiner Liebesglut.

O zärtliches Phantom, umschließe
Mich fest und fester, deinen Mund,
Drück ihn auf meinen Mund—versüße
Die Bitternis der letzten Stund'!

### VI

Du warst ein blondes Jungfräulein, so artig,
So niedlich und so kühl—vergebens harrt ich
Der Stunde, wo dein Herze sich erschlösse
Und sich daraus Begeisterung ergösse—

I heard their weeping and their dying,
And looked on calmly all the while.

I followed their coffins mourning and sighing,
And went to the churchyard as was right;
But afterward, I'm not denying,
I ate my dinner with appetite.

But now I think, with sudden weeping,
Of that dead host beyond recall,
And all at once my heart is leaping
With strange affection for them all.

And mostly Julia's tears are burning
Within my mind as memories stir;
Sorrow turns to wildest yearning,
And day and night I call to her!

In fevered dream, in all her splendor
The dead flower blossoms from the past;
As if in posthumous surrender
She gives herself to me at last.

Oh, let your kiss be wild and stormy,
Tender phantom, give me power
To hold and clasp you—sweeten for me
The bitterness of this last hour!

VI

You were a blonde young lady, well behaved,
So proper and so cool—In vain I craved
The hour when your heart unclosed, revealing
Its depths of inspiration and high feeling—

Begeisterung für jene hohen Dinge,
Die zwar Verstand und Prosa achten g'ringe,
Für die jedoch die Edlen, Schönen, Guten
Auf dieser Erde schwärmen, leiden, bluten.

Am Strand des Rheins, wo Rebenhügel ragen,
Ergingen wir uns einst in Sommertagen.
Die Sonne lachte; aus den liebevollen
Kelchen der Blumen Wohlgerüche quollen.

Die Purpurnelken und die Rosen sandten
Uns rote Küsse, die wie Flammen brannten.
Im kümmerlichsten Gänseblümchen schien
Ein ideales Leben aufzublühn.

Du aber gingest ruhig neben mir,
Im weißen Atlaskleid, voll Zucht und Zier,
Als wie ein Mädchenbild gemalt von Netscher;
Ein Herzchen im Korsett wie 'n kleiner Gletscher.

VII

Vom Schöppenstuhle der Vernunft
Bist du vollständig freigesprochen;
Das Urteil sagt: «Die Kleine hat
Durch Tun und Reden nichts verbrochen.»

Ja, stumm und tatlos standest du,
Als mich verzehrten tolle Flammen—
Du schürtest nicht, du sprachst kein Wort,
Und doch muß dich mein Herz verdammen.

In meinen Träumen jede Nacht
Klagt eine Stimme, die bezichtet

High feeling for those lofty sentiments
Too often scorned by prosy common sense,
Which yet the best and noblest men we know
Give all their dreams and suffering here below.

Along the Rhine's bright shore, where vineyards climb
The hills, we walked one day in summertime.
The sun laughed down; from every flower cup
Love-laden perfumes sweetly drifted up.

The pinks and roses sent us, as we came,
Their scarlet kisses burning like a flame.
And in the meanest daisy on that hour
New life and meaning seemed to come to flower.

But you—you walked on primly at my side,
In satin white, well-bred and dignified,
Just like a girl conceived by Netscher's art—
Beneath your stays, a glacier for a heart.

### VII

Before the court, at Reason's bar,
You've been completely cleared and freed.
The verdict says: The maiden has
Committed no crime by word or deed.

Yes, you stand there silently
While flames consume me as they will—
You do not stir, you do not speak,
And yet my heart condemns you still.

And every night in every dream
A voice rings out that charges you

Des bösen Willens dich und sagt,
Du habest mich zugrund' gerichtet.

Sie bringt Beweis und Zeugnis bei,
Sie schleppt ein Bündel von Urkunden;
Jedoch am Morgen, mit dem Traum,
Ist auch die Klägerin verschwunden.

Sie hat in meines Herzens Grund
Mit ihren Akten sich geflüchtet—
Nur eins bleibt im Gedächtnis mir,
Das ist: ich bin zugrund' gerichtet.

VIII

Ein Wetterstrahl, beleuchtend plötzlich
Des Abgrunds Nacht, war mir dein Brief;
Er zeigte blendend hell, wie tief
Mein Unglück ist, wie tief entsetzlich.

Selbst dich ergreift ein Mitgefühl!
Dich, die in meines Lebens Wildnis
So schweigsam standest, wie ein Bildnis,
Das marmorschön und marmorkühl.

O Gott, wie muß ich elend sein!
Denn sie sogar beginnt zu sprechen,
Aus ihrem Auge Tränen brechen,
Der Stein sogar erbarmt sich mein!

Erschüttert hat mich, was ich sah!
Auch du erbarm dich mein und spende
Die Ruhe mir, o Gott, und ende
Die schreckliche Tragödia.

With ill intent and loudly says
That you've destroyed me through and through.

It brings forth witnesses and proofs,
And pulls out records by the ream;
And when the light of morning dawns
The accuser vanishes with the dream.

With all its facts and documents,
Into my heart it's fled from view—
Only one memory stays with me:
That you've destroyed me through and through.

### VIII

A lightning flash that lit up bright
   The night's abyss, your letter came
   To show as with a sudden flame
How dark my fate, how deep my night

For you felt pity!—it laid its hold
   On you who in my life's dull waste
   Stand like a statue, mute and chaste,
So marble-fair, so marble-cold.

O God, how wretched I must be!
   When even she begins to speak
   And tears roll down that marble cheek,
Even a stone must pity me!

Ah, these were dreadful things to see!
   Have mercy on me, God, and send
   Sweet rest and peace, and make an end—
Oh, end this horrible tragedy.

Die Gestalt der wahren Sphinx
Weicht nicht ab von der des Weibes;
Faselei ist jener Zusatz
Des betatzten Löwenleibes.

Todesdunkel ist das Rätsel
Dieser wahren Sphinx. Es hatte
Kein so schweres zu erraten
Frau Jokastens Sohn und Gatte.

Doch zum Glücke kennt sein eignes
Rätsel nicht das Frauenzimmer;
Spräch es aus das Lösungswort,
Fiele diese Welt in Trümmer.

Es sitzen am Kreuzweg drei Frauen,
Sie grinsen und spinnen,
Sie seufzen und sinnen;
Sie sind gar häßlich anzuschauen.

Die erste trägt den Rocken,
Sie dreht die Fäden,
Befeuchtet jeden;
Deshalb ist die Hängelippe so trocken.

Die zweite läße tanzen die Spindel;
Das wirbelt im Kreise,
In drolliger Weise;
Die Augen der Alten sind rot wie Zindel.

The real Sphinx was like a woman,
Though upon a larger scale;
Lion paws and shape were added
By some old wives' fairy tale.

Dark as death is the enigma
That the real Sphinx poses. Yes,
Dame Jocasta's son and consort
Had an easier one to guess.

Their own riddle even women
Haven't guessed—for which, three cheers!
If it leaked, the world would tumble
All in ruins round our ears.

At the crossroads three women sit:
    They're sighing and spinning,
    They're brooding and grinning;
They're ugly to see as imps from the pit.

The first spins the wheel awry;
    The distaff is threaded,
    Each line is wetted—
Therefore her drooping lips are so dry.

The second lets spindles dance;
    They whirl in rings—
    Droll little things;
The old woman's eyes are red as fire-ants:

Es hält die dritte Parze
In Händen die Schere,
Sie summt Miserere;
Die Nase ist spitz, drauf sitzt eine Warze.

O spute dich und zerschneide
Den Faden, den bösen,
Und laß mich genesen
Von diesem schrecklichen Lebensleide!

## XI

Mich locken nicht die Himmelsauen
Im Paradies, im sel'gen Land;
Dort find ich keine schönre Frauen,
Als ich bereits auf Erden fand.

Kein Engel mit den feinsten Schwingen
Könnt mir ersetzen dort mein Weib;
Auf Wolken sitzend Psalmen singen,
Wär auch nicht just mein Zeitvertreib.

O Herr! ich glaub, er wär das beste,
Du ließest mich in dieser Welt;
Heil nur zuvor mein Leibgebreste,
Und sorge auch für etwas Geld.

Ich weiß, es ist voll Sünd' und Laster
Die Welt; jedoch ich bin einmal
Gewöhnt, auf diesem Erdpechpflaster
Zu schlendern durch das Jammertal.

Genieren wird das Weltgetreibe
Mich nie, denn selten geh ich aus;

The third of the Fates holds shears;
    She hums the dreary
    Chant *Miserere*;
Her nose is pointed, a wart appears.

Oh, speed the wheel, and sever
    This thread for me,
    And set me free
From this life's frightful affliction forever!

## XI

Those heavenly pastures tempt me not,
Nor holy realms in Paradise;
The women there are a lovely lot
But the ones on earth are just as nice.

No angel with fine wings for limbs
Can substitute for my own wife;
Sitting on clouds and singing hymns
Is not my view of The Good Life.

Dear Lord, just leave me here below,
I think it would be none the worse;
But cure my ailments first, you know,
And spare some money for my purse.

I know the world is full of sin
And vice, but still through all these years
I've gotten used to strolling in
This asphalt-pavement vale of tears.

The world's to-do won't bother me,
I seldom stir outside to roam;

In Schlafrock und Pantoffeln bleibe
Ich gern bei meiner Frau zu Haus.

Laß mich bei ihr! Hör ich sie schwätzen,
Trinkt meine Seele die Musik
Der holden Stimme mit Ergötzen.
So treu und ehrlich ist ihr Blick!

Gesundheit nur und Geldzulage
Verlang ich, Herr! O laß mich froh
Hinleben noch viel schöne Tage
Bei meiner Frau im statu quo!

At my wife's side I like to be
In robe and slippers here at home.

Leave me with her! To hear her voice
Go prattling on like a babbling brook
Is sweetest music—I rejoice.
How true and honest is her look!

Just health and extra cash—Lord, give
No more than that, please! Oh, bestow
A brace of more good days to live
Beside my wife in statu quo!

# Himmelfahrt

Der Leib lag auf der Totenbahr',
Jedoch die arme Seele war,
Entrissen irdischem Getümmel,
Schon auf dem Wege nach dem Himmel.

Dort klopft' sie an die hohe Pforte,
Und seufzte tief und sprach die Worte:
«Sankt Peter, komm und schließe auf!
Ich bin so müde vom Lebenslauf—
Ausruhen möcht ich auf seidnen Pfühlen
Im Himmelreich, ich möchte spielen
Mit lieben Englein Blindekuh
Und endlich genießen Glück und Ruh'!"

Man hört Pantoffelgeschlappe jetzund,
Auch klirrt es wie ein Schlüsselbund,
Und aus einem Gitterfenster am Tor
Sankt Peters Antlitz schaut hervor.

Er spricht: «Es kommen die Vagabunde,
Zigeuner, Polacken und Lumpenhunde,
Die Tagediebe, die Hottentotten—
Sie kommen einzeln und in Rotten,
Und wollen in den Himmel hinein
Und Engel werden und selig sein.
Holla! Holla! Für Galgengesichter
Von eurer Art, für solches Gelichter
Sind nicht erbaut die himmlischen Hallen—
Ihr seid dem leidigen Satan verfallen.

## Ascension

The body lay upon the bier;
The poor soul was already clear
Of earthly tumult, on its way
To Heaven on that very day.

It knocked upon the lofty gate,
Sighed, and began to expatiate:
"St. Peter, come, unlock this place!
I am so weary of life's race—
I'd like to rest on silken stuff
In Heaven's realm, play blindman's buff
With sweet little angels midst the Blest,
And taste at last of blissful rest."

Now shuffling slippers sounded near,
A bunch of keys was jingling clear;
A gateside window opened wide,
And there St. Peter peered outside.

He said: "We get a lot of tramps,
Gypsies, Polacks, rogues, and scamps,
Loafers, louts, and Hottentots—
Some come singly, some in lots—
They all want in; their stock request
Is: Make us angels, and Heaven-blest.
Away, away! for such a crew,
For gallows birds that look like you,
The halls of Heaven have no room—
You're Satan's meat till crack of doom.

Fort, fort von hier! und trollt euch schnelle
Zum schwarzen Pfuhle der ewigen Hölle—"

So brummt der Alte, doch kann er nicht
Im Polterton verharren, er spricht
Gutmütig am Ende die tröstenden Worte:
«Du arme Seele, zu jener Sorte
Halunken scheinst du nicht zu gehören—
Nu! Nu! Ich will deinen Wunsch gewähren,
Weil heute mein Geburtstag just
Und mich erweicht barmherzige Lust—
Nenn mir daher die Stadt und das Reich,
Woher du bist; sag mir zugleich,
Ob du vermählt warst?—Eh'liches Dulden
Sühnt oft des Menschen ärgste Schulden;
Ein Eh'mann braucht nicht in der Hölle zu schmoren,
Ihn läßt man nicht warten vor Himmelstoren."

Die Seele antwortet: «Ich bin aus Preußen,
Die Vaterstadt ist Berlin geheißen.
Dort rieselt die Spree, und in ihr Bette
Pflegen zu wässern die jungen Kadette;
Sie fließt gemütlich über, wenn's regent—
Berlin ist auch eine schöne Gegend!
Dort bin ich Privatdozent gewesen,
Und hab über Philosophie gelesen—
Mit einem Stiftsfräulein war ich vermählt,
Doch hat sie oft entsetzlich krakeelt,
Besonders wenn im Haus kein Brot—
Drauf bin ich gestorben und bin jetzt tot."

Sankt Peter rief: «O weh! o weh!
Die Philosophie ist ein schlechtes Metier.
Wahrhaftig, ich begreife nie,

So toddle off! Go dash pellmell
Into the pit of eternal Hell."—

The Ancient growled, but couldn't maintain
The blustering tone; he spoke again
Some words of solace good-naturedly:
"Poor soul, you do not seem to be
That other sort of scamp, I'd say.
Well, well! I'll grant your wish today,
For it's my birthday—I'm inclined
To have a soft heart and lenient mind.
Now tell me what town and country you
Are from; and kindly tell me, too,
If you are married, for conjugal woes
May atone for the worst of sins, God knows.
Husbands don't roast in Hell, or wait
Like other mortals at Heaven's gate."

"I am from Prussia," the soul put in.
"My native town is called Berlin.
The Spree rolls through, and in its bed
The young cadets make water, it's said.
The rains make it overflow, like as not—
Berlin is sure a lovely spot!
I was an instructor there, you see,
And busily studied philosophy.
I married a canoness—my mistake:
She quarreled fiercely without a break,
Above all, when the house lacked bread—
That did me in, and now I'm dead."

Cried Peter: "Alas! I am afraid
Philosophy is a wretched trade.
To tell the truth, I cannot see

Warum man treibt Philosophie.
Sie ist langweilig und bringt nichts ein,
Und gottlos ist sie obendrein;
Da lebt man nur in Hunger und Zweifel,
Und endlich wird man geholt vom Teufel.
Gejammert hat wohl deine Xantuppe
Oft über die magre Wassersuppe,
Woraus niemals ein Auge von Fett
Sie tröstend angelächelt hätt—
Nun, sei getrost, du arme Seele!
Ich habe zwar die strengsten Befehle,
Jedweden, der sich je im Leben
Mit Philosophie hat abgegeben,
Zumalen mit der gottlos deutschen,
Ich soll ihn schimpflich von hinnen peitschen—
Doch mein Geburtstag, wie gesagt,
Ist eben heut, und fortgejagt
Sollst du nicht werden, ich schließe dir auf
Das Himmelstor, und jetzo lauf
Geschwind herein—

                    Jetzt bist du geborgen!
Den ganzen Tag, vom frühen Morgen
Bis abends spät, kannst du spazieren
Im Himmel herum und träumend flanieren
Auf edelsteingepflasterten Gassen.
Doch wisse, hier darfst du dich nie befassen
Mit Philosophie; du würdest mich
Kompromittieren fürchterlich—
Hörst du die Engel singen, so schneide
Ein schiefes Gesicht verklärter Freude—
Hat aber gar ein Erzengel gesungen,
Sei gänzlich von Begeistrung durchdrungen,
Und sag ihm, daß die Malibran
Niemals besessen solchen Sopran—

Why anyone works at philosophy.
It's boring stuff and doesn't pay,
And also godless, by the way.
You suffer the pangs of hunger and doubt,
Till the devil hauls you down and out.
I suppose your Xantippe nagged without stop
About soup so thin there wasn't a drop
Of fat that might have smilingly eyed her
Before it gratefully slid inside her.
Cheer up, poor soul, and comfort you!
I have strict orders, it is true,
On anyone of whom we learn
He made philosophy his concern,
Above all, the godless German brand—
I drive him off roughly, out of hand.
But as I said, my birthday's today,
And so you won't be chased away;
I'll open Heaven's gate for you;
Now shake a leg and hurry through,
But quick——

        "And now you're safe at last!
From morn to night till day is past,
You're free to dream and stroll throughout
The halls of Heaven, and gad about
On gem-paved street and jeweled lane.
But mind, here you must clear your brain
Of all philosophy; else, you see,
You'll compromise me dreadfully.
When angels sing, screw up your face
To register ecstatic grace;
If an archangel sings, be sure to say
That rapture carries you quite away,
That Malibran did not rejoice

Auch applaudiere immer die Stimm'
Der Cherubim und der Seraphim,
Vergleiche sie mit Signor Rubini,
Mit Mario und Tamburini—
Gib ihnen den Titel von Exzellenzen
Und knickre nicht mit Reverenzen.
Die Sänger, im Himmel wie auf Erden,
Sie wollen alle geschmeichelt werden—
Der Weltkapellenmeister hier oben,
Er selbst sogar, hört gerne loben
Gleichfalls seine Werke, er hört es gern
Wenn man lobsinget Gott dem Herrn
Und seinem Preis und Ruhm ein Psalm
Erklingt im dicksten Weihrauchqualm.

Vergiß mich nicht. Wenn dir die Pracht
Des Himmels einmal Langweile macht,
So komm zu mir; dann spielen wir Karten.
Ich kenne Spiele von allen Arten,
Vom Landsknecht bis zum König Pharo.
Wir trinken auch—Doch apropos!
Begegnet dir von ungefähr
Der liebe Gott, und fragt dich: woher
Du seiest? so sage nicht: aus Berlin,
Sag lieber: aus München, oder aus Wien."

In such a rich soprano voice;
Applaud whenever you hear a hymn
By cherubim or seraphim,
Compare their voices to Signor Rubini's,
To Mario's, or Tamburini's;
Always address them 'Your Excellence,'
And bow extra low with reverence;
For singers, in Heaven as down below,
All want to be flattered in gobs, you know.
The Cosmic Conductor himself, up here,
Just loves to hear the listeners cheer
One of his works, and is never bored
To hear praises sung to God the Lord,
Or glorifying psalms bawled loud
With incense thick as any cloud.

"Keep me in mind. Heaven's glory may
Get you a little bored some day,
So look me up; we'll play cards here.
I know all kinds of games, no fear,
From lansquenet to aces-high.
We'll drink as well. Oh, by the by,
If you run into the Lord, dear chum,
And if he asks you whence you come,
Don't say Berlin—why, use your head,
Say Munich or Vienna instead."

## Diesseits und Jenseits des Rheins

Sanftes Rasen, wildes Kosen,
Tändeln mit den glühnden Rosen,
Holde Lüge, süßer Dunst,
Die Veredlung roher Brunst,
Kurz, der Liebe heitre Kunst—
Da seid Meister ihr, Französen!

Aber wir verstehn uns baß,
Wir Germanen, auf den Haß.
Aus Gemütes Tiefen quillt er,
Deutscher Haß! Doch riesig schwillt er,
Und mit seinem Gifte füllt er
Schier das Heidelberger Faß.

## This and That Side of the Rhine

Wild caresses, tender throes,
Toying with a burning rose,
  Fragrant fetor, pretty lies,
  Raw lust in a noble guise,
  Love's glad arts in any wise—
Ah, you French have mastered those!

But we Germans bow to none
When there's hating to be done.
  German hate! it swells and spills
  From the soul in giant rills,
  And its poison overfills
Even Heidelberg's great tun.

## An Meinen Bruder Max

Max! Du kehrst zurück nach Rußlands
Steppen, doch ein großer Kuhschwanz
Ist für dich die Welt: Pläsier
Bietet jede Schenke dir.

Du ergreifst die nächste Grete,
Und beim Klange der Trompete
Und der Pauken, dum! dum! dum!
Tanzest du mit ihr herum.

Wo dir winken große Humpen,
Läßt du gleichfalls dich nicht lumpen,
Und wenn du des Bacchus voll,
Reimst du Lieder wie Apoll.

Immer hast du ausgeübet
Luthers Wahlspruch: Wer nicht liebet
Wein und Weiber und Gesang—
Bleibt ein Narr sein Leben lang.

Möge, Max, das Glück bekränzen
Stets dein Haupt und dir kredenzen
Täglich seinen Festpokal
In des Lebens Kuhschwanzsaal!

## To My Brother Max

Max, you are returning to
Russia's steppes, but life for you
Is a romping rub-a-dub-dub:
Pleasure beckons from every pub.

There you grab some Gretchen who
Happens to be next to you,
Drums go bang and trumpets bawl,
And you dance her round the hall.

Where there's foam to top a cup,
There you're sure to live it up,
And when Bacchus lends you fire,
You sing like Apollo's lyre.

You have practised hitherto
Luther's motto: Someone who
Loves not women, wine and song—
Stays a fool his whole life long.

Max, may fortune crown your days,
Proffer brimming cups always,
Keep you ever safe from strife,
In the dancing hall of life.

Wenn sich die Blutegel vollgesogen,
Man streut auf ihren Rücken bloß
Ein bißchen Salz, und sie fallen ab—
Doch dich, mein Freund, wie werd ich dich los?

Mein Freund, mein Gönner, mein alter Blutsauger,
Wo find ich für dich das rechte Salz?
Du hast mir liebreich ausgesaugt
Den letzten Tropfen Rückgratschmalz.

Auch bin ich seitdem so abgemagert,
Ein ausgebeutet armes Skelett—
Du aber schwollest stattlich empor,
Die Wänglein sind rot, das Bäuchlein ist fett.

O Gott, schick mir einen braven Banditen,
Der mich ermordet mit raschem Stoß—
Nur diesen langweil'gen Blutegel nicht,
Der langsam saugt—wie werd ich ihn los?

11

When leeches have sucked their fill of blood,
To get them off, some salt will do—
A bit on their backs and down they drop—
But friend, how shall I get rid of you?

My friend, my patron, my old bloodsucker:
The right salt for you—what will it be?
My last salt drop of spinal marrow,
You've sucked it out so lovingly.

And I have grown so thin since then,
A wasted skeleton and weak---
But you have swelled to portly size,
Fat in the belly and red in the cheek.

Oh God, let me be murdered by
Some good old bandit, brisk and grim,
But not this slow-sucking tiresome leech—
How shall I get rid of him?

Den Strauß, den mir Mathilde band
Und lächelnd brachte, mit bittender Hand
Weis ich ihn ab—Nicht ohne Grauen
Kann ich die blühenden Blumen schauen.

Sie sagen mir, daß ich nicht mehr
Dem schönen Leben angehör,
Daß ich verfallen dem Totenreiche,
Ich arme unbegrabene Leiche.

Wenn ich die Blumen rieche, befällt
Mich heftiges Weinen—Von dieser Welt
Voll Schönheit und Sonne, voll Lust und Lieben,
Sind mir die Tränen nur geblieben.

Wie glücklich war ich, wenn ich sah
Den Tanz der Ratten der Opera—
Jetzt hör ich schon das fatale Geschlürfe
Der Kirchhofratten und Grabmaulwürfe.

O Blumendüfte, ihr ruft empor
Ein ganzes Ballett, ein ganzes Chor
Von parfümierten Erinnerungen—
Das kommt auf einmal herangesprungen,

Mit Kastagnetten und Zimbelklang,
In flittrigen Röckchen, die nicht zu lang;
Doch all ihr Tändeln und Kichern und Lachen,
Es kann mich nur noch verdrießlicher machen!

I

Mathilde brings me a bouquet
Smiling the while—I wave it away
With pleading hands. Only with dread
Can I see flowers blooming red.

These tell me I belong no more
To life's fair muster as before,
I, poor unburied corpse, a prey
Forfeit to the Dark Prince's sway.

When I smell flowers, I must fall
To weeping. For this world has all
Of sun and splendor, life and cheer—
What's left for me is but a tear

How happy I was to see of yore
The opera rats of the ballet corps—
But now I can hear the shuffling that's
The dreadful sound of the churchyard rats.

O flowery fragance, you recall
A whole ballet, a chorus all
Perfumed with memories that sing—
They come on suddenly with a spring,

In tinseled skirts, not overlong,
Castanets clash, the cymbals bong—
But every giggle and spangle and frill
Can only make me sadder still.

Fort mit den Blumen! Ich kann nicht ertragen
Die Düfte, die von alten Tagen
Mir boshaft erzählt viel holde Schwänke—
Ich weine, wenn ich ihrer gedenke.—

Away with the flowers! I cannot bear
These scents that speak with spiteful air
Of days as sparkling as a gem—
I weep, I weep to think of them.

Dich fesselt mein Gedankenbann,
Und was ich dachte, was ich sann,
Das mußt du denken, mußt du sinnen—
Kannst meinem Geiste nicht entrinnen.

Ein gar subtiler Spiritus
Ist dieser Geist, ein Dominus
Im Geisterheer vom höchsten Range;
Ihn ehrt sogar die Muhme Schlange.

Stets weht dich an sein wilder Hauch,
Und wo du bist, da ist er auch;
Du bist sogar im Bett nicht sicher
Vor seinem Kusse und Gekicher!

Mein Leib liegt tot im Grab, jedoch
Mein Geist, er ist lebendig noch
Und wohnt gleich einem Hauskobolde
In deinem Herzchen, meine Holde!

Vergönn das traute Nestchen ihm,
Du wirst nicht los das Ungetüm,
Du wirst nicht los den kleinen Schnapphahn,
Und flöhest du bis China, Japan.

Denn überall, wohin du reist,
Sitzt ja im Herzchen dir mein Geist;
Hier träumt er seine tollsten Träume,
Hier schlägt er seine Purzelbäume.

I

My spirit binds you as with steel,
And what I think and what I feel,
That you must think, in my control—
You never can escape my soul.

Of all the spirits under the sun,
This soul's a very subtle one,
A soul of master rank—to wit,
Even cousin serpent honors it.

You feel its wild breath over you,
And where you are, there it is too;
Even in bed you're powerless
Before its whispering caress.

Dead in the grave my body lies—
My soul lives on and never dies;
It dwells like a house-familiar here
Within your little heart, my dear!

Grant it the cozy nest to dwell:
You can't escape this imp of Hell.
You can't escape this highwayman
By fleeing to China or Japan.

So everywhere, in every part,
My soul abides still in your heart;
It dreams its maddest dreams right there,
It leaps and somersaults in thin air.

Hörst du, er musizieret jetzt—
Die Flöh' in deinem Hemd ergötzt
So sehr sein Saitenspiel und Singen,
Daß sie vor Wonne hochaufspringen.

Listen, it's making music now—
Its lyre and songs so delight somehow
The fleas in your blouse that, by and by,
In raptured joy they spring up high.

Laß mich mit glühenden Zangen kneipen,
Laß grausam schinden mein Gesicht,
Laß mich mit Ruten peitschen, stäupen—
Nur warten, warten laß mich nicht!

Laß mit Torturen aller Arten
Verrenken, brechen mein Gebein,
Doch laß mich nicht vergebens warten,
Denn warten ist die schlimmste Pein!

Den ganzen Nachmittag bis sechse
Hab gestern ich umsonst geharrt—
Umsonst; du kamst nicht, kleine Hexe,
So daß ich fast wahnsinnig ward.

Die Ungeduld hielt mich umringelt
Wie Schlangen;—jeden Augenblick
Fuhr ich empor, wenn man geklingelt,
Doch kamst du nicht—ich sank zurück!

Du kamest nicht—ich rase, schnaube,
Und Satanas raunt mir ins Ohr:
„Die Lotosblume, wie ich glaube,
Mokiert sich deiner, alter Tor!"

## IV

Let pincers nip my flesh red-hot,
Let me be flayed from sole to pate,
Or whipped with scourges—but do not
Make me just wait and wait and wait!

Let tortures mangle me anew
With broken bones and twists and sprains,
But don't make me vainly wait for you,
For waiting is the worst of pains.

I looked for you all yesterday
In vain, till six was left behind:
You little witch, you came not—nay,
I almost went out of my mind.

Impatience held me tightly bound
Like coiling serpents—I would start
Each time I heard the doorbell's sound,
But you came not—down sank my heart!

You did not come—I rage and fume,
And Satan whispers in ridicule:
"The lotus flower, we can presume,
Is laughing at you, you old fool!"

## Die Schlesischen Weber

Im düstern Auge keine Träne,
Sie sitzen am Webstuhl und fletschen die Zähne:
»Deutschland, wir weben dein Leichentuch,
Wir weben hinein den dreifachen Fluch—
    Wir weben, wir weben!

Ein Fluch dem Gotte, zu dem wir gebeten
In Winterskälte und Hungersnöten;
Wir haben vergebens gehofft und geharrt,
Er hat uns geäfft und gefoppt und genarrt—
    Wir weben, wir weben!

Ein Fluch dem König, dem König der Reichen,
Den unser Elend nicht konnte erweichen,
Der den letzten Groschen von uns erpreßt,
Und uns wie Hunde erschießen läßt—
    Wir weben, wir weben!

Ein Fluch dem falschen Vaterlande,
Wo nur gedeihen Schmach und Schande,
Wo jede Blume früh geknickt,
Wo Fäulnis und Moder den Wurm erquickt —
    Wir weben, wir weben!

Das Schiffchen fliegt, der Webstuhl kracht,
Wir weben emsig Tag und Nacht—
Altdeutschland, wir weben dein Leichentuch,
Wir weben hinein den dreifachen Fluch,
    Wir weben wir weben!«

## *The Silesian Weavers*

In somber eyes no tears of grieving;
Grinding their teeth, they sit at their weaving:
"O Germany, at your shroud we sit,
We're weaving a threefold curse in it—
　　We're weaving, we're weaving!

"A curse on the god we prayed to, kneeling
With cold in our bones, with hunger reeling;
We waited and hoped, in vain persevered,
He scorned us and duped us, mocked and jeered—
　　We're weaving, we're weaving!

"A curse on the king of the rich man's nation
Who hardens his heart at our supplication,
Who wrings the last penny out of our hides
And lets us be shot like dogs besides—
　　We're weaving, we're weaving!

"A curse on this false fatherland, teeming
With nothing but shame and dirty scheming,
Where every flower is crushed in a day,
Where worms are regaled on rot and decay—
　　We're weaving, we're weaving!

"The shuttle flies, the loom creaks loud,
Night and day we weave your shroud—
Old Germany, at your shroud we sit,
We're weaving a threefold curse in it,
　　We're weaving, we're weaving!"